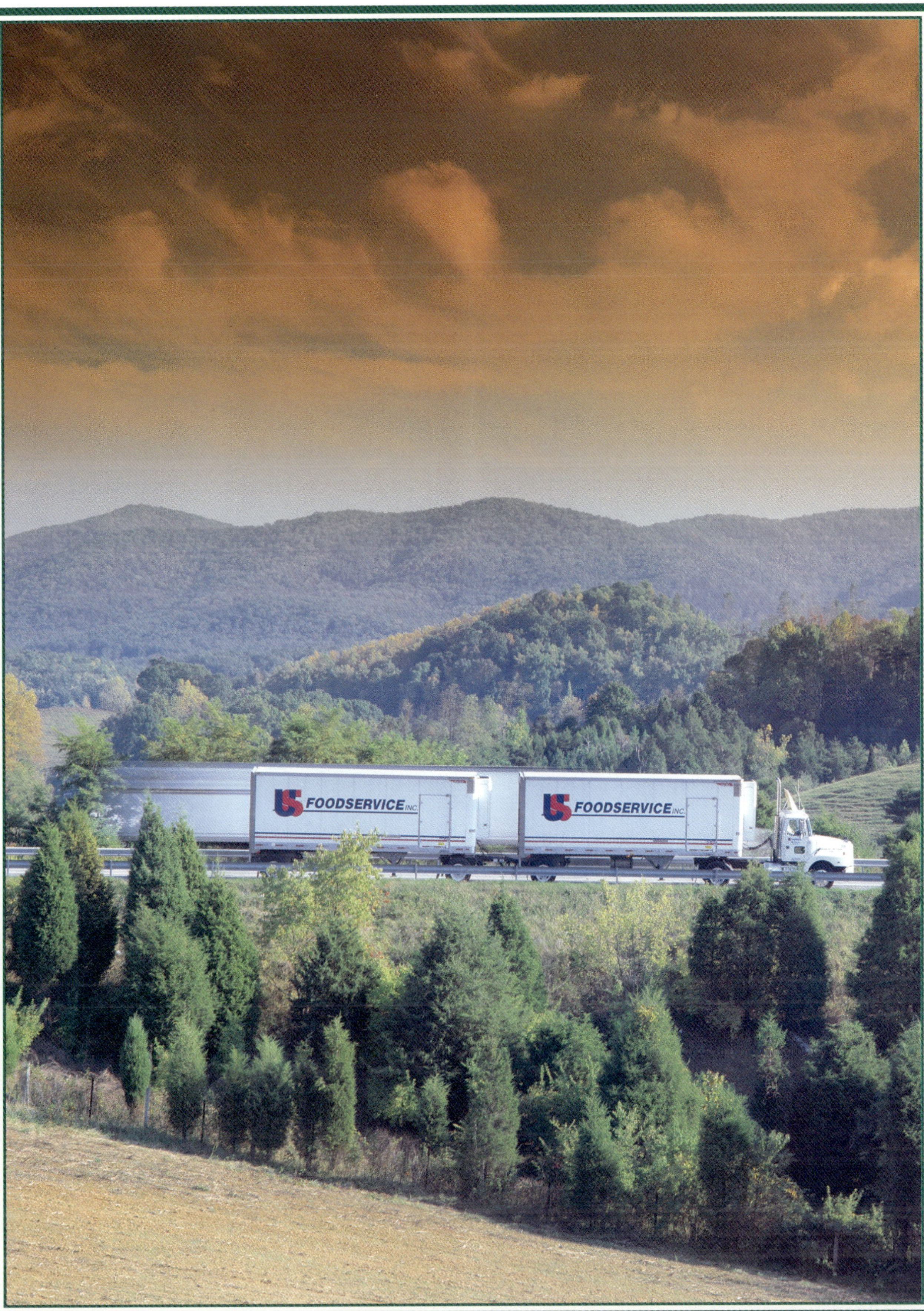

FOODSERVICE INC.

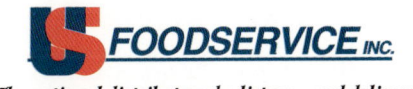

The national distributor who listens. . .and delivers!™

CHICAGO DIVISION

US FOODSERVICE and its employees are committed to developing partnerships with customers, partnerships based on hard work and trust.

US FOODSERVICE is a company that delivers—to its customers, to its employees, to its vendors—choices, resources, satisfaction, service, commitment.

The US FOODSERVICE, Chicago Division, has a proud heritage dating back to 1883 when the John Sexton & Company, now US FOODSERVICE, was founded.

John Sexton, responding to customers' requests for larger food container products in the early years, developed the #10 can, which later became the standard for the industry. Today, US FOODSERVICE, Chicago Division, continues to set industry standards designed to help its customers.

Over the years, the US FOODSERVICE, Chicago Division, has consistently provided its customers with the extra value and service needed to help grow their businesses. US FOODSERVICE has always understood that its customers' success assures the company's success.

Today, our product lines include fresh produce, fresh boxed beef, an outstanding line of frozen and dry grocery items, imported and specialty foods, paper and janitorial supplies and more than five thousand equipment and supply products.

To better serve you, we are currently expanding another warehouse and tripling our cooler space. This expansion is possible because of your support of our product lines and will allow the addition of fresh chicken, fresh liquid milk, fresh ground beef and new specialty produce items.

Our well-trained sales representatives can assist you in menu planning and food cost analysis using their state-of-the-art laptop computers. Additionally, they will make sure that what you purchase from us is best suited for your specific needs.

US FOODSERVICE, Chicago Division, customer services include:

❖ RS/PC-A computer link between your PC and our host computer, allowing direct order entry, menu costing and inventory control.

❖ Foodservice contract and design services to assist you in building or remodeling.

❖ A complete ware-washing program, including dishwashers and laundry with twenty-four-hour service.

❖ Healthcare services managed by our healthcare director, including the source tech software system providing nutritional analysis, inventory and ordering, plus cost control.

Most importantly, it is the relationship between you and our employees that helps grow our businesses. We can possess the finest buildings, equipment and products, but without the best people, those things are useless. At US FOODSERVICE, Chicago Division, our team of more than three hundred employees has over two thousand years of collective foodservice experience, and it's all available to help you become a more successful foodservice operator.

As a locally oriented, yet nationally linked distributor organization and the third largest national foodservice distributor in the country, US FOODSERVICE delivers—with a personal touch—unparalleled service capabilities and total commitment to the business success of its customers. The superb collection of nationally branded product recipes on the following pages continues our tradition of helping you, our customer, operate more successfully and profitably.

US FOODSERVICE's full line of food and non-food products is your source for everything you need to operate an efficient and profitable foodservice operation.

US FOODSERVICE

PRESENTS

Recipes For Today's Menus

Copyright © 1996 US FOODSERVICE

All rights reserved. No part of this book may be reproduced in any form or by any means in another book without the written permission of the publisher or authors, except when permitted by law.

ISBN: 1-879234-43-2

Library of Congress Catalog No. 96-078931

Published by Heritage Publishing, Inc., 1720 Regal Row, Suite 228, Dallas, Texas, 75235. Phone: 214-630-4300

US FOODSERVICE
Marketing Coordinator   Jill Swenson

HERITAGE PUBLISHING

Publisher	Rodney L. Dockery
Editorial Director	Caleb Pirtle III
Executive Editor	Kenneth E. Lively
Production Editor	Marnie Burkett
Staff Writer	Bob Perkins Jr.
Editorial Assistant	Leigh Ann Linney
Art Director	Janet Bergin Todd
Book Designer	Mary Catherine Kozusko
Cover Photography	Mark V. Davis/Davis Studios

Vice President Corporate Sales   Darrell Pesek

Printed by The Bidal Group: David Terrazas, president.

Manufactured in the United States of America.

First Printing

CONTENTS

BREAKFAST 1

APPETIZERS & SALADS 9

SOUPS & SANDWICHES 19

MEATS 31

SEAFOOD 43

POULTRY 53

SIDE DISHES & BREADS 61

PIZZA & PASTA 69

DESSERTS 79

BREAKFAST

Breakfast Biscuit Sticks, page 2

Breakfast Burritos

Breakfast Biscuit Sticks

BREAKFAST BURRITOS

Yield: 10 servings

36	ounces STOUFFER'S® Creamed Chipped Beef, thawed and divided	1/4	teaspoon salt
1/2	cup sour cream	1/4	teaspoon McCORMICK Black Pepper
1/2	cup milk	1/2	teaspoon hot pepper sauce (optional)
10	eggs, lightly beaten	2	tablespoons butter or margarine
2	tablespoons water	10	flour tortillas
5	tablespoons chopped green onion, divided	1/3	cup diced tomato
1	cup grated Cheddar cheese, divided		

- Preheat standard oven to 375 degrees. Grease a 12" x 20" baking dish.
- To make sauce, in a large bowl combine 3/4 of creamed chipped beef and all of sour cream and milk. Spread 1/2 cup of sauce in prepared baking dish. Set aside remaining sauce.
- In a large bowl, combine eggs, water, 2 tablespoons green onion, 1/2 cup grated Cheddar cheese, salt, black pepper and hot pepper sauce.
- Melt butter in large skillet. Add egg mixture and scramble until eggs are set. Fold in remaining creamed chipped beef.
- Divide the egg mixture evenly among the 10 tortillas. Fold two opposite edges of each tortilla over the filling.
- Place tortillas seam side down in baking dish. Cover with remaining sauce. Top with remaining 1/2 cup grated Cheddar cheese, remaining 3 tablespoons green onion and diced tomato.
- Bake 20-25 minutes or until cheese is melted.

BREAKFAST BISCUIT STICKS

Yield: 165 sticks
Serving size: 1 ounce

5	cups cold water (50 degrees)	1	dozen eggs, soft scrambled
1	box GOLD MEDAL® Buttermilk Biscuit Mix	1	tablespoon McCORMICK Coarse Black Pepper
2	cups grated cheese		Melted butter
2	cups diced ham		

- Combine all ingredients except butter in large mixing bowl. Mix using a rubber spatula until a soft dough forms.
- Follow package directions for rolling out dough to 1/2" thick.
- Using a pastry wheel, cut dough into 1" x 3" strips. Transfer strips to paper-lined or greased sheet pan.
- Follow baking time and temperatures as listed on package. Brush baked biscuit sticks with melted butter.

BREAKFAST

BREAKFAST PIZZA

Yield: 6 servings

2	cups biscuit mix	3	eggs
1/2	cup cold water	2	tablespoons milk
1	pound JIMMY DEAN® Brick Sausage, cooked, crumbled and drained	1/2	teaspoon salt
		1/8	teaspoon McCORMICK Pepper
1	cup LAMB-WESTON Hash Brown Potatoes, thawed	1	cup grated Cheddar cheese

❖ Mix biscuit mix and water to form a soft dough. Pat dough into 12" pizza pan.
❖ Spoon sausage over dough. Sprinkle with hash brown potatoes. Beat eggs, milk, salt and pepper; pour over top. Sprinkle with cheese.
❖ Bake at 400 degrees until crust is golden and eggs are set—about 20-25 minutes.

Variations: Add onions and mushrooms or green and red bell peppers.

BREAKFAST TO BRUNCH BAKE

Yield: 40 servings
Serving size: 4 ounces

2	cups diced onion
2	cups diced green pepper
1/2	cup butter
4	pounds frozen LAMB-WESTON Hash Brown Potatoes
1	#10 can BRYAN Ham Shanks (6 pounds, 8 ounces), drained* and chopped
4	dozen eggs, beaten
1	teaspoon McCORMICK Black Pepper

❖ Sauté onion and green pepper in butter.
❖ Place all ingredients in a large bowl and mix well.
❖ Bake in an oiled, full steam table pan at 350 degrees for 40 minutes or until set.

*Reserve ham shank juices for soups, stews or cooking rice.

MEXICAN SUNRISE SANDWICH

Yield: 1 sandwich

	Salsa
1	medium egg
1	3" diameter JIMMY DEAN Sausage Patty
1	AWREY Thaw & Serve Pre-sliced, Traditional or Country Hy 3" Biscuit
	Pepper cheese, grated
	Mild jalapeño pepper

❖ Mix 1/2 teaspoon salsa in with egg; fry within a 3" diameter grill ring. Grill sausage patty. Butter and lightly grill the cut sides of both biscuit slices.
❖ On bottom biscuit slice, place grilled egg and sausage patty, spoon additional salsa over top and sprinkle with grated cheese.
❖ Rest biscuit top over sandwich. Garnish with mild jalapeño pepper.

WHOLE WHEAT BREAKFAST BAGEL

Yield: 1 serving

1	ARNIE'S Whole Wheat Bagel, thawed
2	tablespoons margarine, divided
2	large eggs, beaten
2	slices HORMEL Ham
2	slices American or Cheddar cheese
	Cantaloupe, fresh strawberries and parsley

❖ Split bagel in half and toast; set aside.
❖ Melt 1 tablespoon margarine in fry pan. Pour in eggs. Cook over low heat, stirring occasionally, until it reaches desired consistency. Remove from pan; keep warm.
❖ Melt remaining tablespoon margarine in same fry pan. Sauté ham until lightly browned and hot.
❖ To make sandwich, place a slice of ham on each cut side of toasted bagel. Place scrambled eggs on top of ham on bottom half of bagel. Top egg with cheese. Cover with top half of bagel, ham facing cheese. Serve immediately.
❖ Garnish with slices of cantaloupe, fresh strawberries and parsley on plate.

HAWAIIAN SUNRISE OATMEAL

Yield: 19 servings
Serving size: 1 cup

1	quart, 2 cups water	2	cups chopped RYKOFF-SEXTON Mandarin Oranges, well-drained
1	quart, 2 cups reconstituted FLORIDA'S NATURAL Orange Juice	1 1/2	cups brown sugar
1	quart, 1 1/4 cups uncooked QUAKER Kettle Hearty Oats	2	cups coconut
1 1/2	teaspoons salt (optional)		Toasted coconut
1	quart crushed pineapple, well-drained		

❖ Bring water and orange juice to boil in 8-quart heavy saucepan. Add oats and salt; return to boil. Reduce heat; simmer, uncovered, 8 minutes or until most of liquid is absorbed.

❖ Fold pineapple, oranges, brown sugar and coconut into prepared oatmeal. Transfer to steam table; cover tightly. Hold on medium (#5) setting.

❖ Let stand 30 minutes before serving.

❖ Garnish with toasted coconut.

Time-saving tip: Prepare oatmeal 24 hours in advance; hold in refrigerator. Reheat oatmeal; add additional ingredients just before serving.

Holding time: 1/2 hour in steam table (#5 setting) or warming cabinet.

TAFFY APPLE OATMEAL

Yield: 19 servings
Serving size: 1 cup

1	gallon water
1	quart, 3 cups uncooked QUAKER Kettle Hearty Oats
2	teaspoons salt (optional)
2	cups MRS. RICHARDSON'S Fat-Free Caramel Topping
1 1/2	cups RYKOFF-SEXTON Apple Pie Filling
	Apple slices

❖ Bring water to boil in 8-quart heavy saucepan. Add oats and salt; return to boil. Reduce heat; simmer, uncovered, 8 minutes or until most of liquid is absorbed.

❖ Fold caramel topping and pie filling into prepared oatmeal. Transfer to steam table; cover tightly. Hold on medium (#5) setting.

❖ Let stand 30 minutes before serving.

❖ Garnish with a few apple slices in each corner of pan.

Time-saving tip: Prepare oatmeal 24 hours in advance; hold in refrigerator. Reheat oatmeal; add additional ingredients just before serving.

Holding time: 1/2 hour in steam table (#5 setting) or warming cabinet.

TANGY FRUIT AND NUT MUESLI

Yield: 30 servings
Serving size: 1 cup

1	gallon, 2 cups peeled, seeded and chopped oranges	2	tablespoons McCORMICK Ground Cinnamon
2	quarts, 2 1/2 cups water		Milk, cream or yogurt (optional)
2	quarts uncooked QUAKER Old-Fashioned Oats		Orange slices
3	cups pitted, diced dates		Pitted, diced dates
3	cups coarsely chopped walnuts		

❖ Combine all ingredients in large mixing bowl. Refrigerate, covered, overnight.

❖ Transfer to 2-quart soup liner. Serve cold* with milk, cream or yogurt, if desired.

❖ Garnish with orange slices and dates in center of muesli.

❖ May be held in refrigerator 32-40 degrees up to 5 days.

❖ Hold over ice during entire serving time.

*May be served hot, if desired.

BREAKFAST

Hawaiian Sunrise, Taffy Apple, Peach-N-Pecan Oatmeal

PEACH-N-PECAN OATMEAL

Yield: 16 servings
Serving size: 1 cup

1	gallon water	2	teaspoons McCORMICK Cinnamon
1	quart, 3 cups uncooked QUAKER Kettle Hearty Oats		Cream or milk (optional)
1	teaspoon salt (optional)		Chopped pecans, toasted
3	cups RYKOFF-SEXTON Diced Peaches, drained		
1½	cups brown sugar		
1⅓	cups chopped pecans, toasted		

- ❖ Bring water to boil in 8-quart heavy saucepan. Add oats and salt; return to boil. Reduce heat; simmer, uncovered, 8 minutes or until most of liquid is absorbed.
- ❖ Fold peaches, brown sugar, pecans and cinnamon into prepared oatmeal. Transfer to steam table; cover tightly. Hold on medium (#5) setting. Serve with cream or milk, if desired.
- ❖ Let stand 30 minutes before serving.
- ❖ Garnish with toasted pecan pieces over top of oatmeal.

Variation: Substitute diced, drained pears for peaches.
Time-saving tip: Prepare oatmeal 24 hours in advance; hold in refrigerator. Reheat oatmeal; add additional ingredients just before serving.
Holding time: ½ hour in steam table (#5 setting) or warming cabinet.

HONEYED FRUIT AND NUT SPREAD

Yield: 24 servings
Serving size: 1½ ounces

1½	cups honey
2½	pounds CROSS VALLEY FARMS Cream Cheese
3	ounces dried apricots, finely chopped
3	ounces walnuts, finely chopped

- ❖ Beat together honey and cream cheese.
- ❖ Add apricots and walnuts until thoroughly combined.

Serving tip: Spread on muffins, biscuits, English muffins, bagels, toast and quick breads.

BREAKFAST

KELLOGG'S® LOWFAT GRANOLA PANCAKES

Yield: 6 pancakes

1	cup all-purpose flour
1	tablespoon sugar
2	teaspoons baking powder
1/4	teaspoon salt
2	cups KELLOGG'S® Lowfat Granola, divided
1	cup skim milk
1	egg
2	tablespoons vegetable oil

- In large bowl, combine flour, sugar, baking powder, salt and 1 cup granola. Set aside.
- In second bowl, beat together milk, egg and oil. Add to flour mixture, stirring until combined.
- Pour about 1/3 cup of batter on hot griddle coated with cooking spray. Cook until golden brown on both sides. Top each pancake equally with remaining cup of granola.

CHERRY-PEAR UPSIDE-DOWN COFFEECAKE

Yield: 24 servings

6	ounces KELLOGG'S® Corn Flakes® Cereal		21	ounces tart cherry pie filling
1 1/2	cups firmly packed brown sugar		1	pound, 7 ounces buttermilk biscuit mix
2	ounces nuts, coarsely chopped		1	cup sugar
1/4	cup melted margarine or butter		1/4	cup margarine or butter, softened
1	tablespoon cinnamon		3	eggs
1	(9 ounce) can pears, drained and chopped		1 1/4	cups milk

- In mixer bowl, using flat beater attachment, combine cereal, brown sugar, nuts, margarine and cinnamon until thoroughly mixed. Sprinkle about 3 cups cereal mixture over bottom of greased 18" x 13" sheet pan; set remaining cereal aside.
- Spread pears evenly over mixture in pan. Dot with cherry filling, set aside.
- In mixer bowl, on low speed, mix together biscuit mix, sugar, margarine, eggs and milk until combined. Spread evenly over cereal-fruit mixture in pan. Sprinkle with remaining cereal mixture.
- Bake at 350 degrees about 40 minutes or until wooden pick inserted near center comes out clean. Cool slightly before serving. To serve, turn piece upside-down before placing on plate.

COCOA BANANA MUFFINS

Yield: 4 dozen

2	pounds all-purpose flour		3/4	cup vegetable oil
1	pound, 2 ounces sugar		1	pound, 14 ounces ripe bananas, sliced
1 1/2	teaspoons salt			Vegetable cooking spray
1/4	cup baking powder			
1 1/2	teaspoons baking soda			*Coffee Sauce*
1 1/2	cups unsweetened cocoa powder		2	cups sugar
14	ounces KELLOGG'S® All Bran® Cereal		3/4	cup all-purpose flour
4 1/2	cups skim milk		1	quart evaporated skim milk
10	egg whites		1	quart prepared coffee

- Combine flour, sugar, salt, baking powder, baking soda and cocoa powder. Set aside.
- Combine cereal and milk in mixer bowl. Let stand about 3 minutes or until cereal softens.
- Add egg whites and oil. Mix on low speed, with flat beater attachment, until all ingredients are well-combined. Stir in bananas. Add dry ingredients; mix on low speed only until combined. Spray muffin pan; using #12 scoop, portion batter in 2 3/4" cups.
- Bake at 400 degrees about 20 minutes or until lightly browned.
- For coffee sauce, in 4-quart saucepan, stir together sugar and flour. Gradually add milk and coffee, stirring until smooth. Cook over medium heat, stirring constantly, until mixture starts to boil. Continue cooking and stirring 1 minute longer.
- Serve muffins with warm coffee sauce.

BREAKFAST

Potato Basil Frittata

Savory Brunch Flautas with Eggs, Chilies and Cheese

POTATO BASIL FRITTATA

Yield: 3 (12") frittatas, 18 servings

1	(3 pound) bag LAMB'S SUPREME® IQF Hash Browns (S69)*		Pepper
1½	cups chopped onions	3	ounces sun-dried tomatoes, soaked and chopped
36	large eggs, beaten	6	tablespoons chopped fresh basil
	Salt	1½	cups grated Parmesan cheese

❖ For each frittata, in greased 12" skillet, cook hash browns and ½ cup onions 5 minutes, turning to brown.
❖ Pour 3 cups eggs in skillet. Top with 1 ounce tomatoes and 2 tablespoons basil. Cook over medium heat, lifting egg mixture around edges to allow uncooked portions to flow underneath. Cook about 6 minutes or until egg mixture is almost set.
❖ Sprinkle with 1 ounce cheese. Place under broiler, cheese melter or salamander 1-2 minutes or until cheese melts and top is lightly browned. Cut into 6 wedges and serve.

*May use other Lamb Weston IQF Shredded Hash Browns.

SAVORY BRUNCH FLAUTAS WITH EGGS, CHILIES AND CHEESE

Yield: 18-24 servings

	Cooking spray	2	cups diced red bell pepper
2	quarts fresh or frozen corn kernels	1½	cups melted butter
8	large eggs, lightly whipped	2	pounds jack cheese, grated and divided
1	quart sour cream	30	FERNANDO'S FOODS Fiesta Supreme™ Shredded
2	cups cornmeal		Chicken (2.25 ounce) Flautas
8	ounces canned green chilies		

❖ Spray full-size hotel pan or large Texas-style muffin tins with non-stick cooking spray.
❖ In large bowl, combine corn, eggs, sour cream, cornmeal, chilies, red pepper and butter. Mix ingredients together, stir in 1½ pounds cheese.
❖ Fill hotel pan or muffin tins halfway with egg-cheese mixture. Place chicken flautas side by side on top and cover with remaining mixture.
❖ Bake at 375 degrees for 50-60 minutes until golden; sprinkle with remaining ½ pound cheese during last 15 minutes of cooking.

Serving suggestion: Serve alongside mixed green salad drizzled with vinaigrette.

APPETIZERS & SALADS

Spinach and Sausage Stuffed Mushrooms, page 12

WISCONSIN CHEESE SAUCE WITH THREE ROASTED PEPPERS
(TRES CHILIES QUESO ASADO)

1	small red onion, finely chopped	1	cup whole milk
1/2	cup butter	1	pound Wisconsin part-skim mozzarella cheese, grated
24	Anaheim peppers, roasted, peeled, seeded and sliced into thin strips	1	pound seeded plum tomatoes, diced
		2	cups roasted fresh corn (cut from cob)
5	Poblano peppers, roasted, peeled, seeded and sliced into thin strips	2	cups tortilla chips
		8	sprigs cilantro leaves
6	Serrano peppers, roasted, peeled, seeded and minced	40	corn, flour or whole wheat tortillas, warmed
2	cups Wisconsin Crema Mexicana		

- ❖ Sauté onion in butter in saucepan. Stir in peppers; cook 1 minute.
- ❖ Add Wisconsin Crema Mexicana and milk; bring to boil.
- ❖ Reduce heat to low; stir in cheese. Cook until sauce thickens and cheese melts.
- ❖ Divide cheese sauce among serving bowls. Top with tomato, corn, tortilla chips and cilantro.
- ❖ Serve tortillas alongside sauce. Have guests spread sauce onto tortillas.

Variations: Upscale—Serve sauce with firm fish or seafood, such as tuna.
Serve sauce with colorful tortillas, including red (made with red chilies), green (made with spinach), yellow (made with yellow corn) and blue (made with blue corn).
Midscale—Serve sauce over grilled chicken or turkey breasts.
Snack—Serve sauce with purchased tortilla chips.
Brunch—Spoon sauce over an omelet; top with a dollop of sour cream and garnish with salsa and sliced avocados.

CHILI DIP

Yield: 8-10 servings

1	(8 ounce) package cream cheese
1	cup STOUFFER'S® Chili Con Carne, heated
1/3	cup salsa
1/3	cup grated CROSS VALLEY FARMS Cheddar cheese
1/4	cup sliced black olives
1/4	cup chopped green onion
	Tortilla chips or corn chips

- ❖ Place block of cream cheese on a serving platter. Top cream cheese with the hot chili, salsa, Cheddar cheese, black olives and green onion.
- ❖ Serve with tortilla chips or corn chips.

Wisconsin Cheese Sauce with Three Roasted Peppers

Chili Dip

APPETIZERS & SALADS

ROSARITA'S CHILES RELLENOS

Yield: 20 servings

1	#2 1/2 can ROSARITA'S® Whole Green Chilies (1 pound, 11 ounces), drained
20	3" x 1/2" strips Cheddar cheese and/or Monterey Jack cheese (1 pound, 4 ounces)
1/2	cup all-purpose flour
6	whole eggs, separated
1/2	teaspoon salt
	WESSON® CRYSTAL® Shortening
	ROSARITA'S® Mild Green Chili Salsa

- *Dry outside of chilies well.*
- *Insert one cheese strip into each green chile.*
- *Roll stuffed chilies in flour.*
- *In bowl, beat egg whites until stiff.*
- *Fold in egg yolks and salt.*
- *In deep fat fryer or skillet, heat oil to 350 degrees. Dip each stuffed chile into egg batter, coating well. Fry until golden, turning once.*
- *Drain.*
- *Serve hot with salsa or your favorite chile relleno sauce.*

SAUSAGE STUFFED MUSHROOMS

Yield: 24 appetizers

24	large mushrooms
1	medium onion
1/2	pound LA BELLA VILLA Bulk Italian Sausage
1	medium garlic clove, finely minced
1	cup Italian bread crumbs
1/3	cup grated Parmesan cheese
2	tablespoons chopped parsley
1/2	cup chicken broth

- *Wash mushrooms. Remove stems and chop. Drain.*
- *Sauté onion, sausage, garlic and bread crumbs. Mix cheese and parsley. Stir together with chicken broth and sautéed items. Stuff mushroom caps.*
- *Bake at 325 degrees for 25 minutes, uncovered, in shallow pan with 1/4" water covering bottom of pan.*

LEMON DILL SEAFOOD SPREAD

Yield: 4 cups

2	(8 ounce) packages CROSS VALLEY FARMS Light Cream Cheese, softened
1/2	cup lemon butter dill cooking sauce
3/4	cup thinly sliced green onions (reserve 1/4 cup to garnish)
1/2	teaspoon McCORMICK Lemon Pepper Seasoning
2	cups thoroughly drained NICHEREI Lobster Meat, Flaked Crab Meat or coarsely chopped Surimi Seafood (1 pound)
	Fresh dill
	KEEBLER Crackers or Melba Toast

- *Combine cream cheese, cooking sauce, green onions and seasoning. Stir in seafood. Press mixture into 4-cup mold lined with plastic wrap or dampened cheesecloth. Cover and chill 4 hours or overnight.*
- *Unmold and garnish with fresh dill or green onions. Serve with crackers or melba toast.*

APPETIZERS & SALADS

Crab Spinach Dip

Spinach and Sausage Stuffed Mushrooms

CRAB SPINACH DIP

Yield: 10 cups

1	(64 ounce) container STOUFFER'S® Spinach Artichoke Dip, thawed
1/2	pound crabmeat, flaked
8	green onions, chopped
1/8	cup lemon juice
1	teaspoon hot sauce (optional)
	Toasted baguette slices or tortilla chips

❖ Preheat oven to 350 degrees. Grease 2 shallow, 3-quart baking dishes.

❖ In a large bowl, combine all ingredients. Spoon into prepared baking dishes.

❖ Bake uncovered for 20-30 minutes or until thoroughly heated. Serve with toasted baguette slices or tortilla chips.

SPINACH AND SAUSAGE STUFFED MUSHROOMS

24	ounces STOUFFER'S® Spinach Soufflé, thawed
32	ounces STOUFFER'S® Cornbread Dressing, thawed
1	pound Italian-style sausage, thoroughly cooked, drained and crumbled
1/2	cup Parmesan cheese (plus additional to garnish)
5-6	pounds whole white mushrooms, cleaned and stems removed

❖ Preheat standard oven to 400 degrees.

❖ In large bowl, combine spinach soufflé and cornbread dressing.

❖ Add cooked sausage and Parmesan cheese. Stir well.

❖ Place mushrooms on baking sheets and fill with spinach mixture, mounding slightly. Sprinkle with Parmesan cheese.

❖ Bake 10-15 minutes or until cheese and mushrooms are lightly browned.

APPETIZERS & SALADS

GARLIC TOMATO SKIN STRIPS

Yield: 48 appetizers

48	LAMB'S Natural MunchStrips® (N26)		Salt (optional)
2	pounds tomatoes, seeded and chopped		Pepper (optional)
1/3	cup chopped fresh basil	1 1/2	cups grated LA BELLA VILLA Mozzarella Cheese
3/4	teaspoon McCORMICK Garlic Powder	1/3	cup grated Parmesan cheese

❖ Deep-fry potatoes at 350-360 degrees 2 1/2-3 minutes or until golden brown and crisp. Or, heat in standard oven at 425 degrees 14-16 minutes (convection oven at 375 degrees 10-15 minutes).

❖ Combine tomatoes, basil and garlic. Season with salt and pepper, if desired. Fill potatoes with tomato mixture, using 1 heaping tablespoon each. Sprinkle with combined cheeses. Bake at 425 degrees (standard oven) 2-3 minutes or until cheese melts and is lightly browned.

ITALIAN APPETIZER PLATE

Yield: 10 servings
Serving size: 4 1/2 ounces chicken plus
4 ounces appetizer items and 2 ounces sauce

30	TYSON Spicy Breast Tenderloins (#2556)
2 1/2	cups prepared ANGELA MIA Pizza Sauce
1	tablespoon Italian seasoning blend
10	green leaf lettuce leaves
60	roasted red bell pepper strips
50	whole, pitted RYKOFF-SEXTON Black Olives
30	mozzarella cheese cubes (3/4")
20	marinated, drained artichoke heart halves
	Minced parsley

❖ Deep-fry frozen breast tenderloins at 350 degrees for 3-5 minutes. Remove from fryer. Drain. Keep warm.

❖ Prepare pizza sauce by combining sauce and Italian seasoning. Mix well. Heat over low heat for 5-6 minutes or until fully warm. Remove from heat, but keep warm.

❖ To assemble appetizer plates: On lettuce leaves, arrange 6 red bell pepper strips, 5 black olives, 3 mozzarella cubes and 2 artichoke halves on each plate. Sprinkle with minced parsley. Add 3 breast tenderloins and serve with 1/4 cup pizza sauce.

Garlic Tomato Skin Strips

Italian Appetizer Plate

APPETIZERS & SALADS

CARIBBEAN FLAUTAS WITH MANGO SALSA

Yield: 16 servings

32-48	FERNANDO'S FOODS Fiesta Supreme® Shredded Chicken Flautas		
1	quart Mango Salsa		
1 1/3	cups guacamole or sour cream		
	Cilantro sprigs		

Mango Salsa — Yield: 1 quart

3	cups diced mango
3/4	cup diced red pepper
1/2	cup diced red onion
2	jalapeños, diced
1	tablespoon chopped cilantro
	Juice of 2 limes

❖ For each serving: Heat 2-3 flautas according to package instructions in deep fryer or by brushing with vegetable oil and heating in 400-degree oven for 15 minutes. Remove flautas, center on serving plate and top with 2 ounces Mango Salsa. Serve alongside 1 tablespoon guacamole or sour cream and a sprig of cilantro.

Mango Salsa
❖ Combine mango, red pepper, red onion, jalapeños and cilantro. Toss with lime juice; chill.

BLT FRIES

Yield: 1 serving

4	ounces LAMB-WESTON® Stealth Fries® Shoestrings (S30)	1/4	ounce lettuce, shredded
1/2	cup canned cheese sauce, heated	1	ounce tomato, chopped
		1	tablespoon real or imitation bacon bits

❖ Deep-fry potatoes at 350-360 degrees 2-2 1/2 minutes or until golden brown and crisp. Or, heat in standard oven at 425 degrees 16-22 minutes (convection oven at 400 degrees 8-10 minutes).
❖ On plate, arrange hot fries. Ladle cheese sauce in center of fries. Sprinkle with lettuce, tomato and bacon bits. Serve immediately.

CHILE CON QUESO FRIES

Yield: 10 servings
Serving size: 1/4 cup

2	pounds, 8 ounces LAMB'S Seasoned Fries® Ranch Recipe Wedge Cut (R12)*	1/2	cup PACE Picante Sauce
2	cups chopped mushrooms	2	cups grated CROSS VALLEY FARMS Monterey Jack Cheese With Peppers
1/2	cup chopped onions	2	cups grated CROSS VALLEY FARMS Cheddar Cheese
1	tablespoon oil		Milk (optional)

❖ Deep-fry potatoes at 350-360 degrees 3 1/4-3 3/4 minutes or until golden brown and crisp. Or, heat in standard oven at 450 degrees 18-22 minutes (convection oven at 400 degrees 8-12 minutes).
❖ Cook mushrooms and onions in hot oil until tender. Add picante sauce. Stir in cheeses and heat until melted. For a thinner sauce, stir in some milk. Serve over fries or as a dip.

* May use other LAMB-WESTON coated wedge cuts. Cooking instructions may vary.

Chili Con Queso Fries

BLT Fries

APPETIZERS & SALADS

QUICK QUESADILLA BAGELS

Yield: 2 servings
Serving size: 1 bagel half

1/2	cup grated Colby-Jack cheese
1	ARNIE'S Plain, Egg or Sesame Bagel, baked and split
2	tablespoons chopped green onion
1/4	cup thick and chunky salsa

❖ Divide cheese equally between bagel halves. Sprinkle each with half onion. Top each with half salsa.
❖ Broil 1-2 minutes until cheese is melted and salsa is hot. Cut each half into 4 pieces. Serve immediately.

Serving suggestion: Serve with guacamole, tomato wedges and ripe olive slices in center of plate, surrounded by bagel wedges.

PAPAYA SALSA

Yield: 2 cups

1	ripe papaya (1 pound)	1/8	cup coarsely chopped cilantro
1	fresh jalapeño		Zest of lime
1	medium garlic clove, finely minced	1/4	cup fresh lime juice
1/4	cup finely chopped red onion		

❖ Prepare papaya by cutting into 1/4" cubes. Seed and finely chop the jalapeño peppers. Toss all ingredients together gently and leave at room temperature. Serve salsa within 4-6 hours. For overnight storage, refrigerate.

ARNIE'S BAGELICIOUS BAGEL CHIPS

Yield: 30 servings
Serving size: 1 ounce (3 chips)

2	ARNIE'S Plain Bagels, baked	2	teaspoons McCORMICK Garlic (fresh, crushed or powdered)
2	ARNIE'S Sesame Bagels, baked	1 1/2	teaspoons McCORMICK Dried Oregano
2	ARNIE'S Pumpernickel Bagels, baked	1 1/2	teaspoons McCORMICK Dried Basil
2	ARNIE'S Whole Wheat Bagels, baked	1/4	cup grated Parmesan cheese
6	tablespoons BELLAGIO Olive Oil		Parmesan or Romano cheese (optional)
1/4	cup pesto		

❖ Cut bagels into thin slices using #10 setting on electric slicer. Spread evenly onto parchment-lined full sheet pan.
❖ Drizzle olive oil over bagel slices; toss gently on tray. Sprinkle with pesto, garlic, oregano, basil and Parmesan cheese. Toss gently to coat evenly. Bake until crisp and golden, tossing gently halfway through baking time. Sprinkle with additional Parmesan or Romano cheese, if desired, after baking.
❖ Convection oven: 350 degrees, 9-11 minutes, tossing halfway through baking time.*
Standard oven: 400 degrees, 14-16 minutes, tossing halfway through baking time.*
❖ Great as a replacement for potato chips or as a bar snack.
❖ Serve with marinara sauce garnished with fresh basil or oregano.

*Bagel chips will burn if not tossed halfway through baking.

Quick Quesadilla Bagels

Arnie's Bagelicious Bagel Chips

APPETIZERS & SALADS

DIJON CHICKEN WINGS A LA GREQUE

Yield: 12 servings

2	cups lemon juice	1	teaspoon red pepper flakes
3	cups GREY POUPON® Dijon Mustard	1	quart BELLAGIO Olive Oil
2 1/2	tablespoons minced garlic	12	pounds chicken wings
4	teaspoons dried oregano leaf	5	pounds cooked white beans
3	tablespoons lemon zest	1 1/4	cups grated Parmesan cheese, divided
4	teaspoons McCORMICK Black Pepper		Bitter greens

- ❖ For the marinade, in a large bowl combine the lemon juice, mustard, garlic, oregano, lemon zest, black pepper and red pepper flakes; whisk in the olive oil and set aside 3 cups for the dip. Pour remaining mixture over chicken wings and marinate for 1 hour. After 1 hour, remove wings from marinade and grill or broil until crisp and cooked through; keep warm for service.
- ❖ To prepare bean dip, puree beans with 1 cup Parmesan cheese and reserved marinade; refrigerate for service.
- ❖ For each serving, place 1 pound of chicken wings in a hot oven until warm; remove from oven and serve with 3/4 cup dip placed in an 8-ounce ramekin. Sprinkle wings with 1 teaspoon Parmesan cheese and garnish with bitter greens.

MEDITERRANEAN SALAD

Yield: 12 servings

1 1/4	pounds romaine lettuce, torn into bite-sized pieces	3/4	cup crumbled CROSS VALLEY FARMS Feta Cheese
1	cup sliced RYKOFF-SEXTON Black Olives	1 1/2	cups low-calorie vinegar and oil dressing

- ❖ Combine lettuce and olives in large bowl. Toss well. Cover and chill.
- ❖ To serve, portion 1 1/2 cups lettuce mixture on plate. Sprinkle with 1 tablespoon feta cheese and 2 tablespoons salad dressing.

GOLD SLAW

Yield: 50 servings
Serving size: 1/2 cup

4	cups RYKOFF-SEXTON Mayonnaise	7	pounds cabbage, shredded
1	cup CATTLEMEN'S Gold Sauce	1 1/2	cups grated carrots
1	tablespoon celery seed		

- ❖ Mix mayonnaise, sauce and celery seed together. Combine with cabbage and carrots. Serve chilled.

HONEY MUSTARD VINAIGRETTE

Yield: 100 servings

<u>Honey Mustard Magic</u>

2	cups honey	2	tablespoons salt
2	cups Dijon mustard or brown mustard	1	tablespoon pepper
2 1/3	cups lemon juice	1 1/2	quarts plus 1/3 cup vegetable oil
		1/4	cup poppy seeds (optional)

- ❖ Combine honey and mustard until smooth.
- ❖ Beat together 3 3/4 cups honey mustard magic and remaining ingredients until thoroughly combined.

Dijon Chicken Wings a la Greque

Southwestern Chicken Caesar Salad

APPETIZERS & SALADS

SOUTHWESTERN CHICKEN CAESAR SALAD

Yield: 50 servings

19	pounds romaine lettuce, chopped		
25	ounces fresh cilantro, chopped		
50	TYSON Broiled Chicken Breasts, sliced		
12	ounces OLD EL PASO Taco Seasoning		
3	quarts PROGRESSO Black Beans, drained and rinsed		
3	quarts diced tomatoes		
25	ounces green onions, sliced		
1 1/2	quarts RYKOFF-SEXTON Whole Kernel Corn		
1 1/2	quarts OLD EL PASO Chopped Green Chilies		
3	pounds Cheddar cheese, grated		
4 3/4	quarts *Southwestern Caesar Dressing*		
3	pounds *Tortilla Straw*		
200	purple kale leaves		

Southwestern Caesar Dressing   Yield: 4 3/4 quarts

3	quarts Caesar dressing
2	ounces OLD EL PASO Taco Seasoning
7	cups OLD EL PASO Salsa Mexicana

Tortilla Straw

48	OLD EL PASO 6" Corn Tortillas

- Sprinkle chicken breasts with taco seasoning and grill to order.
- Place all ingredients except chicken, purple kale, Southwestern Caesar Dressing and Tortilla Straw in a stainless steel bowl; gently toss.
- Garnish plates with purple kale, and place tossed salad in the center. Slice the cooked chicken breast into 5 slices and shingle over top of salad. Garnish with Tortilla Straw and serve.

Southwestern Caesar Dressing
- Combine all ingredients together with a wire whisk and refrigerate until needed.

Tortilla Straw
- Cut tortillas crosswise, 1/4" wide to make long, thin strips.
- Place in deep fat fryer at 350 degrees and fry for approximately 1 minute or until they begin to brown.
- Place in a bowl lined with a towel and cover until needed.

Note: Tortilla Straw can be made before serving time and held at room temperature.

GRILLED TURKEY AND SPINACH SALAD WITH WISCONSIN COTIJA CHEESE CROUTONS

Yield: 2 servings
Serving size: 12 ounces

Grilled Turkey

1/4	cup BELLAGIO Olive Oil
2	tablespoons lime juice
1	tablespoon minced garlic
	McCORMICK Salt
	McCORMICK Pepper
1/4	cup pimento, roasted and finely chopped
8	ounces raw PINE RIDGE FARMS Turkey Breast, sliced 1/4" thick

Wisconsin Cotija Cheese Croutons

2	ounces Wisconsin Cotija Cheese
	Peanut oil

6	ounces spinach leaves, torn
1	plum tomato, diced
1/4	cup corn, roasted
1/4	cup roasted pimento (cut into slivers)

Dressing

6	tablespoons BELLAGIO Extra Virgin Olive Oil
1	tablespoon lemon juice
1	tablespoon lime juice
1	tablespoon apple cider vinegar
1/2	teaspoon minced garlic
	McCORMICK Salt
1/4	cup minced cilantro leaves
1	small red onion, sliced 1/4" thick
	McCORMICK Pepper

- Whisk together olive oil, lime juice, garlic, salt and pepper to taste. Stir in pimento. Pour over seasoned turkey slices. Cover and marinate 1 hour. Grill turkey and cut into thin diagonal slices.
- To make croutons, cut cheese into 1/2" cubes. Fry in 3 inches hot peanut oil (380 degrees) 30 seconds or until golden brown.
- Whisk together olive oil, lemon juice, lime juice, vinegar, garlic, salt and pepper. Stir in cilantro.
- Grill onion until just softened. Marinate in dressing 1 hour.
- Remove onion from dressing; set aside.
- Toss spinach with dressing. Divide onto serving plates.
- Arrange turkey slices, onion slices, tomato, corn and pimento on spinach. Sprinkle with croutons.

Variations: Upscale–Substitute firm fish or seafood, such as tuna or swordfish, for the turkey. Serve with a side of cheese bread made with Wisconsin Asadero or Queso Quesadilla.

Midscale–Substitute chicken for the turkey. For the cheese, use Queso Fresco crumbled over top.

APPETIZERS & SALADS

Grilled Turkey and Spinach Salad with Wisconsin Cotija Cheese Croutons

Mediterranean Chicken Salad

MEDITERRANEAN CHICKEN SALAD

Yield: 12 servings

2	pounds TYSON Fully Cooked ³⁄₄" Diced White Fryer Meat, thawed (#3002)*	2	tablespoons cayenne pepper sauce
1	quart prepared cracked bulgur wheat	1¹⁄₂	tablespoons dried mint leaves
3	cups diced cucumbers	¹⁄₂	tablespoon mustard powder
3	cups diced tomatoes	12	whole tomatoes
2	cups minced green onions	12	Boston lettuce leaves
1	cup chopped parsley	12	green onions
1	cup RYKOFF-SEXTON Italian Dressing	36	KEEBLER Rye-Flavored Crackers

❖ Combine chicken, bulgur wheat, cucumbers, tomatoes, green onions and parsley in bowl. Mix well.
❖ Whisk together Italian dressing, pepper sauce, mint leaves and mustard powder in small bowl. Pour over chicken mixture. Toss well. Cover and chill.
❖ Core tomatoes. Cut each tomato into wedges without slicing through bottom. Spread wedges apart to form a cup. Place on lettuce leaf. Fill with chicken mixture.
❖ Serve with a green onion and 3 crackers.
❖ For volume table service, stuff Mediterranean Chicken Salad in tomatoes and keep refrigerated until ready to serve.
❖ For buffet service, line platter with lettuce leaves and spoon on Mediterranean Chicken Salad. Garnish with tomato wedges, black olives and fresh parsley sprigs.

*Can substitute #3138 TYSON Fully Cooked Diced Fryer Leg Meat, ¹⁄₂"; #20697 TYSON Marinated Fajita Steak for a healthful southwestern fajita salad or #1572 TYSON Original Tenderloin. Spoon vegetable-bulgur mixture on top of salad greens and top with crisp tenderloin. Serve additional salad dressing on the side.

CHICKEN CAESAR RICE SALAD

Yield: 32 servings
Serving size: 1 cup

1	box NEAR EAST Rice Pilaf (2 pounds, 4 ounces), uncooked	4¹⁄₂	cups grated carrot
3	pounds boneless TYSON Chicken Breast, cooked and thinly sliced	²⁄₃	cup grated Parmesan cheese
		¹⁄₃	cup RYKOFF-SEXTON Lemon Juice
1³⁄₄	cups sliced ripe pitted olives		Romaine lettuce or purple kale
2	cups RYKOFF-SEXTON Caesar Salad Dressing		Croutons

❖ Prepare rice according to package directions; except omit margarine or butter. Cool in full sheet pan in refrigerator.
❖ Transfer to large mixing bowl. Combine chilled rice with chicken, olives, dressing, carrots, cheese and juice. Toss lightly until all ingredients are well-combined. Refrigerate 3-4 hours.
❖ Serve chilled rice salad over romaine lettuce or purple kale. Sprinkle with croutons; serve additional dressing on the side.

Variation: Substitute turkey breast for chicken breast.
Time-saving tip: Prepare rice 24 hours in advance. Cool rice to 45 degrees or below within 4 hours in shallow pans with a product depth of less than 2 inches in refrigerator. Stir frequently.
Holding time: Hold in cold unit at 45 degrees or below for 3 hours.

APPETIZERS & SALADS

SOUPS & SANDWICHES

Open-Faced Marinated Steak Sandwich, page 25

Pueblo Black Bean Chili

Roasted Garlic Potato Soup

PUEBLO BLACK BEAN CHILI

Yield: 25 servings
Serving size: 1 cup

3	pounds JENNIE-O® Fully Cooked Pulled White Turkey or JENNIE-O® Ground Turkey	3	tablespoons McCORMICK Oregano Leaves
1/4	cup vegetable oil	3	tablespoons McCORMICK Chili Powder
3/4	pound onions, chopped	1/2	tablespoon McCORMICK Ground Allspice
1	tablespoon minced garlic	3	pounds canned black beans, drained
3/4	pound green bell pepper, chopped	1	pound frozen whole kernel corn
3	quarts diced tomatoes (undrained)	1	tablespoon salt
1	quart RYKOFF-SEXTON Tomato Sauce	1/2	teaspoon McCORMICK Cayenne Pepper
3	tablespoons McCORMICK Ground Cumin	1	pound lowfat CROSS VALLEY FARMS Monterey Jack Cheese, grated

- ❖ For pulled turkey: thaw and coarsely chop in food chopper or by hand; set aside.
  For ground turkey: thaw and sauté in stockpot with onions.
- ❖ Heat oil in stockpot. Add onions. Sauté until onions are tender.
- ❖ Stir in prepared turkey, garlic, green pepper, tomatoes, tomato sauce, cumin, oregano, chili powder and allspice.
- ❖ Simmer, covered, for 45 minutes, stirring occasionally.
- ❖ Add drained black beans and corn; simmer, uncovered, an additional 30 minutes.
- ❖ Season with salt and cayenne pepper to taste.
- ❖ At time of service, top each bowl of chili with 2 tablespoons Monterey Jack cheese.

ROASTED GARLIC POTATO SOUP

Yield: 24 servings
Serving size: 1 cup

4	whole garlic bulbs	1	gallon chicken broth
1	pound HORMEL Bacon, diced	2	bay leaves
1	cup chopped onion	1	quart half and half
1	pound carrots, diced	1/2	cup chopped fresh parsley
1/2	cup all-purpose flour		Freshly ground pepper
1	(5 pound) bag TIME SAVOR® Soup Cubes (S71)		Salt

- ❖ Wrap garlic in foil and roast at 350 degrees for 1 hour or until soft. Cool and press out garlic; set aside.
- ❖ Cook bacon until browned. Add onion and carrots; cook until tender. Add flour, cook 1 minute.
- ❖ Stir in soup cubes, chicken broth and bay leaves. Cook 20 minutes or until potatoes are tender. Add garlic, half and half and parsley. Heat through. Season with pepper and salt to taste.

HAM AND BLACK BEAN SOUP

Yield: 25 servings
Serving size: 12 ounces

1	#10 can RYKOFF-SEXTON Whole Tomatoes* (6 pounds, 6 ounces)	2	cups green pepper
1	#10 can RYKOFF-SEXTON Black Beans (6 pounds, 8 ounces)	1	#10 can BRYAN Ham Steaks (6 pounds, 8 ounces)
2	cups diced onion	2	teaspoons salt
		1	teaspoon McCORMICK Pepper

❖ Mix all ingredients in a large stockpot and bring to a boil. Cover and simmer for 30 minutes.

*May substitute 1 (#10) can rotel tomatoes for the whole tomatoes.

WHITE CHICKEN CHILI

Yield: 24 servings
Serving size: 1 cup

3	cups chopped onion	3/4	teaspoon salt
1	tablespoon minced garlic	1 3/4	teaspoons McCORMICK Cayenne Pepper
1	tablespoon BELLAGIO Olive Oil	1	(50 ounce) can SWEET SUE Diced Boned Chicken
1	#10 can RYKOFF-SEXTON Great Northern or Cannelloni Beans (6 pounds, 6 ounces)	3	cups SWEET SUE Chicken Broth
1 1/2	cups canned diced green chilies (24 ounces)		Monterey Jack cheese
2	tablespoons chopped fresh cilantro		Crushed tortilla chips
4	tablespoons McCORMICK Cumin		Sour cream

❖ Sauté onion and garlic in olive oil in large stockpot. Add the next 8 ingredients and heat through.

❖ To serve: Ladle into soup bowls and garnish with Monterey Jack cheese, crushed tortilla chips and sour cream.

PASTA FAGOLI

Yield: 24 servings

4	large onions, chopped	2	teaspoons McCORMICK Pepper
1/2	cup olive oil	1	tablespoon salt
4	stalks celery, finely chopped	4	(16 ounce) cans cannelloni beans
12	garlic cloves, chopped	1	pound SAN GIORGIO Macaroni, cooked
2	pounds fresh spinach, chopped	1	cup minced black olives
4	(16 ounce) cans whole tomatoes	1	cup LA BELLA VILLA Grated Parmesan Cheese
2	tablespoons crumbled leaf oregano		

❖ Sauté onions in oil until golden brown. Add celery, garlic and spinach and continue to sauté until wilted.

❖ Crush tomatoes by hand and add to onion mixture. Add spices, cover and let simmer for 30-40 minutes.

❖ Drain and rinse beans and add them to tomato mixture, continuing to simmer for 15 minutes. Add cooked macaroni, heat thoroughly and serve. Garnish with chopped olives and grated Parmesan cheese.

Serving suggestion: This is a very thick soup. If desired, you may thin with water or vegetable broth.

SOUPS & SANDWICHES

BARLEY AND LENTIL SOUP

Yield: 24 servings

4	tablespoons BELLAGIO Olive Oil	3	quarts beef broth
3	medium onions, chopped	2 1/2	tablespoons RYKOFF-SEXTON Tomato Paste
5	garlic cloves, chopped	1	quart RYKOFF-SEXTON Crushed Tomatoes
4	carrots, sliced	1 1/4	cups pearl barley
5	stalks celery, chopped	1 1/4	cups lentils
2	red bell peppers, chopped		Salt
10	sun-dried tomatoes, chopped		Pepper
2 1/2	teaspoons dried and crumbled basil	1/3	cup chopped fresh parsley (optional)
1 1/4	teaspoons dried and crumbled oregano		

- ❖ Heat oil in heavy saucepan over medium-high heat. Add onions and garlic; sauté until onions are translucent, about 10 minutes.
- ❖ Add next 6 ingredients. Cook until bell pepper just softens, stirring occasionally, about 6 minutes.
- ❖ Mix in broth, tomato paste and tomatoes. Bring mixture to boil. Stir in barley and lentils. Reduce heat; simmer until barley and lentils are tender, stirring occasionally, about 1 1/2 hours.
- ❖ Thin soup to desired consistency with remaining broth. Season with salt and pepper. Ladle into soup bowls and garnish with parsley, if desired.

SANTA FE POTATO SOUP

Yield: 6 gallons, 96 servings
Serving size: 1 cup

2	pounds butter	1/4	cup McCORMICK Chili Powder
5	cups finely diced onion	2	tablespoons McCORMICK Ground Cumin
1	quart finely diced red bell pepper	4	gallons chicken stock
1	quart finely diced poblano pepper	4	pounds TIME SAVOR® Soup Cubes (S71)
2	cups finely diced celery	1/4	cup salt
1/2	cup minced garlic	2	tablespoons McCORMICK White Pepper
2	pounds flour	1/4	cup chopped fresh cilantro

- ❖ Melt butter over high heat.
- ❖ Add all vegetables and garlic and cook for 10 minutes.
- ❖ Add flour, chili powder and cumin. Reduce heat and cook for 8 minutes.
- ❖ Add chicken stock and whisk until smooth.
- ❖ Add soup cubes, salt and pepper.
- ❖ Simmer for 12 minutes.
- ❖ Add cilantro and mix well before serving.

QUICK SHRIMP GUMBO

Yield: 50 servings
Serving size: 6 ounces

2-4	pounds CLASSIC TUREEN® Condensed Tomato Florentine Soup
3	quarts boiling water
4	pounds rice, par-boiled, cooked and drained
3	pounds BEE GEE Salad Shrimp, thawed
2	pounds okra (cut frozen, blanched or canned)
4	tablespoons McCORMICK Cajun Spice Blend

- ❖ Heat condensed soup in package, per directions.
- ❖ Combine soup and boiling water. Bring to a simmer.
- ❖ Add rice, shrimp and okra.
- ❖ Remove from heat and add Cajun spice blend. Serve hot.

SOUPS & SANDWICHES

"California Dreamin'" Croissant Sandwich

Roast Beef Sandwich with Warm Sautéed Onions

"CALIFORNIA DREAMIN'" CROISSANT SANDWICH

Yield: 1 sandwich

1	AWREY Thaw & Serve Croissant (pre-sliced, traditional or wheat), thawed
3	ounces PINE RIDGE FARMS Smoked Turkey, thinly sliced
1	ounce CROSS VALLEY FARMS Muenster Cheese
	Alfalfa sprouts
	Sunflower seeds
	Radicchio lettuce
	Mayonnaise and spicy mustard
	Avocado wedges
	Cherry tomato

❖ On bottom slice of croissant, layer with folded smoked turkey, cheese, alfalfa sprouts, sunflower seeds and radicchio lettuce.
❖ On top slice of croissant, spread a light amount of mayonnaise and mustard.
❖ Garnish with avocado wedges surrounding a cherry tomato.

ROAST BEEF SANDWICH WITH WARM SAUTÉED ONIONS

Yield: 12 servings

1 1/2	cups A.1.® Original Steak Sauce
3/4	cup sour cream
6	cups sliced onions
	Salt
	Pepper
12	kaiser rolls, split
48	slices HORMEL Roast Beef (42 ounces)

❖ Combine A.1. and sour cream. Sauté onion; season with salt and pepper and keep warm.
❖ For each sandwich, spread 1/2 ounce of A.1. sour cream mixture inside roll. Place 3 1/2 ounces of roast beef on bottom half of roll, top with 3 ounces of warm onion and top half of roll and cut sandwich into quarters.

Variation: Chill the onion and mix with a vinaigrette.

SOUPS & SANDWICHES

BLACK PEPPER PORK LOIN ON SOURDOUGH ONION ROLL WITH WATERCRESS SALAD

Yield: 12 servings

3	pounds HORMEL Boneless Pork Loin	12	onion kaiser rolls, toasted
1 1/2	cups BELLAGIO Olive Oil		Rosemary Aioli
12	garlic cloves, peeled and smashed		
4-5	sprigs rosemary		_Rosemary Aioli_
1	cup crushed black peppercorns		Juice of one lemon
		1/2	teaspoon salt
Salad		1/2	teaspoon pepper
4	bunches watercress	1/4	teaspoon McCORMICK Cayenne Pepper
2	pieces fresh horseradish, peeled and cut into 1" pieces	1	large garlic clove
1/3	cup vinaigrette	2	tablespoons McCORMICK Crushed Rosemary
	Salt	1	cup basil-infused olive oil*
	Pepper		

- Marinate the pork in olive oil, garlic, rosemary and peppercorns for 2 days in the refrigerator. Sear and roast the loin to medium, about 155 degrees internal temperature. Allow to sit for 30 minutes.
- For salad: Chop watercress leaves coarsely, grate horseradish and toss with watercress and vinaigrette. Add salt and pepper to taste. Set aside.
- To serve: Thinly slice pork and reserve. Spread toasted onion rolls with Rosemary Aioli. Place 4 ounces of sliced pork on bread. Serve with watercress salad.

Rosemary Aioli
- In food processor, combine lemon juice, salt, pepper, garlic and cayenne pepper to taste. Slowly run in rosemary and basil-infused olive oil.

*To make basil-infused olive oil, bring 1 cup olive oil to 120 degrees. Add 1/4 cup basil, stems coarsely chopped, and steep until cool. Strain.

CHICKEN FRIED STEAK SANDWICH

Yield: 1 sandwich

4	ounces ADVANCE Chicken Fried Steak	Hoagie bun, sesame bun or rye bread
	MOORE'S Onion Rings	Lettuce
	CROSS VALLEY FARMS Pepper Jack Cheese	Tomato slices
	Dijon mustard	

- Preheat oil to 350-360 degrees. Place frozen steak and onion rings in oil; cook until they float or until internal temperature reaches 160 degrees (3-3 1/2 minutes). Place cheese on cooked steak and melt in microwave. Spread Dijon mustard on bread. Put steak on bread and top with lettuce, tomato slices and onion rings.

Serving suggestion: May be served with French fries and cole slaw.

PHILLY PIZZA STEAK

3	tablespoons sliced mushrooms
4	ounces RYKOFF-SEXTON Deluxe Beef Chip Steak or QUALITY FOODS Flavored Quality Steak
1-2	slices CROSS VALLEY FARMS White American Cheese (mozzarella or provolone may be substituted)
	6" or 7" hinged sub roll or hoagie roll
3	tablespoons HUNT'S Pizza Sauce or Tomato Sauce

- Sauté mushrooms and set aside. Place steak on flat grill at 325 degrees or moderate to high heat for 1-2 minutes. Turn. After steak has been turned, chip by holding with one spatula and "chipping" with a second spatula. As steak finishes cooking, add cheese until it melts. Add sliced mushrooms.
- Place in sub roll, cover with pizza sauce and serve.

SOUPS & SANDWICHES

OPEN-FACED MARINATED STEAK SANDWICH

Yield: 12 servings

24	slices Italian bread, toasted and buttered
3/4	cup grated Parmesan cheese
4	cups red wine
1 1/2	cups A.1.® Original Steak Sauce
3/4	cup half and half
3 3/4	pounds sirloin steak
2 1/4	pounds RYKOFF-SEXTON Button Mushrooms
	Parsley, chopped

❖ Sprinkle buttered side of each slice of toast with Parmesan cheese and flash under broiler.
❖ Reduce wine to approximately 3 cups. Combine A.1. with half and half and stir into reduced wine; simmer until thickened. Set aside and keep warm.
❖ For each sandwich, grill a 5-ounce piece of steak to desired doneness and grill 3 ounces of mushrooms. Slice steak and mushrooms and place on cheese side of bread. Cover steak with 4 ounces of warm red wine sauce and sprinkle with chopped parsley.

Serving suggestion: Serve with a red onion and tomato salad.

GRILLED PETITE PRIME RIB AND SWISS CHEESE SANDWICH

Yield: 12 servings

3/4	cup RYKOFF-SEXTON Mayonnaise
1 1/2	cups A.1.® Thick & Hearty Steak Sauce*, divided
12	club steaks (3 1/4 pounds)
24	(1 ounce) slices CROSS VALLEY FARMS Swiss Cheese
24	slices rye bread, toasted

❖ Combine mayonnaise with 3/4 cup of A.1.
❖ For each sandwich, rub a steak with 1 tablespoon of A.1.; grill to desired doneness and top with 2 slices of Swiss cheese; melt cheese. Spread 3 tablespoons of A.1. mayonnaise on one side of 2 slices of toast. Place steak between the two slices of toast and cut in half.

Serving suggestion: Serve with a new potato salad.
*Also great with A.1.® Original Steak Sauce.

Open-Faced Marinated Steak Sandwich

Grilled Petite Prime Rib and Swiss Cheese Sandwich

SOUPS & SANDWICHES

Little Palm Island Chicken Sandwich

Cha-Cha Chile Chicken Sandwich

LITTLE PALM ISLAND CHICKEN SANDWICH

Yield: 12 servings
Serving size: 8 ounces

2 1/4	pounds frozen TYSON® Original Chicken Strips (#3236)	_Jalapeño-Teri Mayo_	
3	cups thinly sliced green bell pepper	1 1/4	cups mayonnaise
3	cups thinly sliced onion	2 1/2	tablespoons chopped ginger
2	tablespoons vegetable oil, hot	2	tablespoons Dijon mustard
12	green leaf lettuce leaves	1 1/2	tablespoons teriyaki sauce
12	gyros-style pitas	1 1/2	tablespoons sesame oil
12	tomato slices	1	tablespoon rice vinegar
	Jalapeño-Teri Mayo	1	tablespoon minced jalapeño

- Deep-fry chicken strips at 350 degrees for 5-5 1/2 minutes. Remove from fryer. Drain. Keep warm.
- Sauté pepper and onion in oil in skillet over medium-high heat for 10-14 minutes or until vegetables are tender. Remove from heat. Keep warm.
- Place pitas in a single layer on baking sheets. Bake in a preheated conventional oven at 350 degrees for 4-7 minutes or until pitas are warm. Remove from oven. Keep warm.
- To assemble sandwich, layer lettuce leaf, 1/4 cup sautéed vegetables, tomato slice and 3 ounces chicken strips on gyro. Top with 2 tablespoons Jalapeño-Teri Mayonnaise. Wrap gyro around sandwich ingredients to form a cone. Secure with a toothpick. Serve immediately.

Jalapeño-Teri Mayo
- Combine in bowl, mix well, cover and refrigerate.

CHA-CHA CHILE CHICKEN SANDWICH

Yield: 10 servings
Serving size: 3 1/2 ounces chicken plus 4 ounces sandwich ingredients

10	TYSON® Home-Style Chicken Thigh Fillets (#2512)
	Vegetable oil
10	CROSS VALLEY FARMS Monterey Jack Cheese Slices
20	green bell pepper rings, 1/4" thick
10	onion slices, 1/4" thick
10	hamburger buns, warm
1 1/4	cups chile pepper ketchup

- Deep-fry frozen chicken fillets at 350 degrees for 4 1/2-5 1/2 minutes. Remove from fryer. Drain. Keep warm.
- Brush with oil and grill over medium-high heat for 6-8 minutes or until browned. Turn once. Remove from grill. Keep warm.
- To assemble sandwich: Layer 1 slice cheese, 2 green pepper rings and 1 onion slice on bottom bun; add chicken fillet and top with 2 tablespoons chile pepper ketchup.

SOUPS & SANDWICHES

CITY SANDWICH WITH BLUE CHEESE SAUCE

Yield: 48 servings

5 1/4	pounds TYSON Fully Cooked Diced White Fryer Meat (3/4" diced, thawed #3002)*		Red onions, slivered
1	cup lemon juice		Alfalfa sprouts
1/2	cup BELLAGIO Olive Oil	9	pounds carrot sticks
1/3	cup low-sodium soy sauce		Blue Cheese Sauce
1/4	cup sesame seeds, toasted		*Blue Cheese Sauce*
3	tablespoons sesame oil	11	cups RYKOFF-SEXTON Blue Cheese Dressing (fat-free)
3	tablespoons minced garlic	3/4	cup minced green onion
2 1/2	tablespoons honey	3/4	cup minced fresh parsley
2	tablespoons McCORMICK Ground Ginger	2	teaspoons coarse-ground McCORMICK Black Pepper
48	green leaf lettuce leaves	1	teaspoon dried dill
3	quarts chopped tomatoes		Fresh parsley
24	pita rounds, sliced in half and warmed		

- ❖ Combine chicken, lemon juice, olive oil, soy sauce, sesame seeds, sesame oil, garlic, honey and ginger in bowl. Mix well. Cover. Refrigerate.
- ❖ To prepare sandwich, portion lettuce leaf and 1/4 cup tomatoes in each pita half. Drain chicken. Add 1/3 cup chicken mixture. Top with red onion and alfalfa sprouts. Serve with carrot sticks and individual ramekins of Blue Cheese Sauce.

Variations: Layer sandwich components on whole-grain bread or sliced sandwich rolls for easy high-volume serving.

For added menu versatility, use sandwich components to create an entree salad. Layer chicken tossed in sesame-soy dressing and wedged tomatoes over fresh green salad. Top with a drizzle of Blue Cheese Sauce and serve with grilled pita wedges.

Substitute prepared Caesar dressing in the sandwich for a Caesar Chicken Sandwich. Simply layer chicken, lettuce, tomato, red onion and top with Caesar dressing in a grilled pita for this popular, quick-to-fix sandwich.

For a gyro-style sandwich, layer sesame-soy chicken mixture, lettuce, tomato, onion, sprouts and Blue Cheese Sauce on a large warm pita round, roll closed and wrap for take-out menus.

*Can substitute #3112 TYSON Fully Cooked Diced Natural Proportion Chicken, 1/2" diced; #0435 TYSON Fully Cooked Flavor-Redi® Breast Fillets, Grill Flavor or #3351 TYSON Chicken Fajita Strips.

Blue Cheese Sauce

- ❖ Combine all ingredients in bowl. Mix well. Cover. Refrigerate.
- ❖ Serve as a dipping sauce for carrots or as a dressing for City Sandwich.
- ❖ Garnish individual ramekins with parsley.

MEDITERRANEAN PORK ON KAISER

Yield: 12 servings

4	whole HORMEL Pork Tenderloins (3-4 pounds)		*Black Olive Aioli*
6	cloves garlic, minced	1	cup RYKOFF-SEXTON Mayonnaise
4	Spanish onions, thinly sliced	1/4	cup ground black olives
3	tablespoons McCORMICK Black Pepper	2	cloves garlic, minced
3	red bell peppers	2	teaspoons RYKOFF-SEXTON Lemon Juice
6	cups mixed greens (mache, argula, frisee, red oak)	1/4	cup chopped parsley
1/4	cup BELLAGIO Extra Virgin Olive Oil		Salt
1/4	cup balsamic vinegar		Pepper
	Salt		
	Pepper		
12	kaiser rolls		
	Black Olive Aioli		

- ❖ Roll pork tenderloin in garlic, 1/2 the onions and black pepper. Wrap tightly with plastic wrap and marinate in refrigerator overnight.
- ❖ Roast red peppers over flame until skin blisters. Cool and peel. Cut peppers into strips. Grill remaining onion slices. Grill pork tenderloin to medium—about 12-15 minutes. Thinly slice. Toss greens with olive oil, balsamic vinegar and salt and pepper to taste.
- ❖ Cut rolls in half and toast. For each sandwich, spread top and bottom of Kaiser rolls with Black Olive Aioli. Lay 5-6 slices of pork on bottom half. Top with onions, peppers, tossed greens and top of roll.

Serving suggestion: Serve sandwich with potato or vegetable chips.

Black Olive Aioli

- ❖ Combine all ingredients. Mix well, cover and refrigerate.

MEXICAN SEA-WICH

Yield: 24 servings
Serving size: 1 sandwich

24	semolina or other rectangular rolls, split
24	iceberg lettuce leaves
6	pounds tomatoes, sliced into 48 slices
24	(8 ounce) fillets CRISPY STYLE® HPC, cooked according to package directions
2	quarts Black Bean Salsa
4	avocados, peeled and sliced into 48 slices (optional)

<u>Black Bean Salsa</u>

2	pounds cooked black beans, drained
3	cups diced red bell pepper
2	cups chopped scallions
2	cups corn niblets
1	tablespoon seeded and minced jalapeño pepper
1/2	cup lemon juice
1/2	cup olive oil
1/2	cup minced fresh cilantro

- For each sandwich: Split a roll, place a lettuce leaf and 2 tomato slices on roll, and top with prepared HPC portion.
- Spoon 1/3 cup Black Bean Salsa over fish and top with 2 avocado slices, if desired.

Note: This recipe works equally well with ICELANDIC® or SEASTAR® Crispy Style® seafood products.

<u>Black Bean Salsa</u>

- In bowl, combine beans, pepper, scallions, corn, jalapeño peppers and lemon juice; toss. Let stand 15 minutes.
- Stir in oil and cilantro; toss to coat. Cover and let stand at least 2 hours.

CAJUN COD SANDWICH

Yield: 24 servings
Serving size: 1 sandwich

24	(5 ounce) frozen ICELANDIC® Cod Tails
1/2	cup Cajun Spice Blend
24	lettuce leaves
24	hard rolls, split
3	pounds tomatoes, sliced into 24 slices
3	cups Cajun Rémoulade

<u>Cajun Spice Blend</u>

3	tablespoons McCORMICK Paprika
2	tablespoons McCORMICK Onion Powder
1 1/2	tablespoons McCORMICK Thyme Leaves
1	tablespoon McCORMICK Ground Marjoram
2	teaspoons McCORMICK Salt
2	teaspoons McCORMICK Ground Pepper
2	teaspoons McCORMICK Garlic Powder
1 1/2	teaspoons McCORMICK Ground Red Pepper

<u>Cajun Rémoulade</u>

2	cups light mayonnaise
1	cup dill pickle relish
1/2	cup Dijon mustard
1/2	cup chopped fresh parsley
2	tablespoons lemon juice
1	teaspoon hot red pepper sauce

- Sprinkle each frozen fillet with 1 teaspoon Cajun Spice Blend. Bake at 400 degrees 12-14 minutes or until cooked through.
- For each sandwich, place lettuce leaf on base of split roll.
- Top with a tomato slice and spoon on 2 tablespoons Cajun Rémoulade. Place cod tail on top and replace top of roll.

<u>Cajun Spice Blend</u>
- Combine all ingredients.

<u>Cajun Rémoulade</u>
- Combine all ingredients.

MEDITERRANEAN HERO

Yield: 6-8 servings

1	loaf French or sourdough bread
2	tablespoons BELLAGIO Olive Oil
4	ripe tomatoes, chopped
1/2	red onion, diced
2	leaves romaine lettuce, rinsed and patted dry
4	ounces cheese, grated
12	ounces cooked BEE GEE Buffalo Shrimp
2	tablespoons chopped Italian parsley

<u>Wild Buffalo Sauce</u>
Mild:

1/2	cup RYKOFF-SEXTON Mayonnaise
1/2	cup sour cream
1	teaspoon RYKOFF-SEXTON Lemon Juice
6	tablespoons of your favorite hot sauce

Medium:

1/2	cup RYKOFF-SEXTON Mayonnaise
1/2	cup sour cream
1	teaspoon RYKOFF-SEXTON Lemon Juice
8	tablespoons of your favorite hot sauce
1	teaspoon McCORMICK Cayenne Pepper

Hot:

1/2	cup RYKOFF-SEXTON Mayonnaise
1/2	cup sour cream
1	teaspoon RYKOFF-SEXTON Lemon Juice
1/2	cup of your favorite hot sauce
2	teaspoons McCORMICK Cayenne Pepper

- Cut the loaf of bread in half lengthwise, making the bottom half larger. Hollow out halves to create a shell.
- Drizzle olive oil over the bottom half of bread. Layer bread with tomatoes, red onion, lettuce, grated cheese and buffalo shrimp.
- Garnish with parsley.
- To make sauce, combine all ingredients. For extra flavor, serve with sauce, if desired.
- To serve, cut into sandwich-size slices or slice thinly for hors d'oeuvres.

SOUPS & SANDWICHES

Grilled Chicken and Basil Mayonnaise Bagel

Ham Steak Sandwich

CAJUN SWORDFISH BAGEL

Yield: 1 serving

<u>Cajun Mayonnaise</u>
1/3	cup RYKOFF-SEXTON Mayonnaise
1	tablespoon McCORMICK Cajun Seasoning
1	ARNIE'S Onion Bagel, thawed and split
	Iceberg lettuce, finely shredded
2	slices tomato
1	tablespoon margarine
1	(8 ounce) ARCTIC HARVEST Swordfish Fillet, approximately 1" thick, thawed (if frozen) and butterflied
1 1/2	teaspoons Cajun seasoning

- ❖ To make Cajun mayonnaise, combine mayonnaise and Cajun seasoning, mixing well.
- ❖ Toast bagel; spread each half with 1 tablespoon Cajun mayonnaise; set aside.
- ❖ Place lettuce on bottom half of bagel. Top with tomato slices.
- ❖ Melt margarine in sauté pan. Rub both sides of swordfish with Cajun seasoning. Sauté swordfish 3-4 minutes per side or until done. Place cooked swordfish over tomatoes. Cover with top half of bagel, mayonnaise facing fish. Serve immediately.

Serving suggestion: Serve with Spanish rice mixed with black beans.

HAM STEAK SANDWICH

Yield: 12 servings

1 1/2	cups crushed drained pineapple
3	cups A.1.® Original Steak Sauce, divided
2 1/4	pounds ham steak, sliced into 12 slices
24	slices RYKOFF-SEXTON Pineapple Rings
24	slices pumpernickel bread, toasted

- ❖ Combine crushed pineapple and 2 1/4 cups of A.1. in a food processor; puree and set aside.
- ❖ For each sandwich, rub one half steak with 1/2 tablespoon of A.1.; grill. Rub two pineapple rings with 1/2 tablespoon of the A.1.; grill. Spread 3 ounces of pineapple puree on one side of two slices of toast and place ham and pineapple rings on bottom slice of toast. Cover with top slice of toast and cut on a bias in half.

Variation: Substitute pineapple rings with grilled pear slices.

SOUPS & SANDWICHES

HAM FOCACCIA BAGEL

Yield: 1 serving

1	ARNIE'S Plain Bagel, baked	1	teaspoon grated Parmesan cheese
1	tablespoon BELLAGIO Olive Oil	2	slices tomato
2	halves sun-dried tomato, chopped	2	slices LA BELLA VILLA Provolone Cheese
1/4	teaspoon crushed fresh garlic	1	tablespoon margarine
1/8	teaspoon dried basil	3	ounces HORMEL Ham, sliced

- Cut bagel in half. Top each half with equal amounts of olive oil, sun-dried tomatoes, garlic, basil and Parmesan cheese. Cover each half with a tomato slice and a slice of provolone cheese.
- Toast under broiler until cheese is melted.
- Meanwhile, melt margarine in sauté pan. Cook ham until lightly brown and hot. Place ham on bottom half of bagel. Cover with top half of bagel, cheese facing ham. Cut in half. Serve immediately.

Variation: For a vegetarian version of sandwich, omit margarine and ham. Place both slices of tomato on bottom half of bagel. Proceed as directed above.

VEGETABLE BAGEL FINGER SANDWICH

Yield: 1 serving

1	ARNIE'S Marble Bagel, baked and cooled		*Garden Vegetable Cream Cheese*
4	tablespoons *Garden Vegetable Cream Cheese*	1	pound CROSS VALLEY FARMS Cream Cheese
1	ounce cucumber, sliced	1/2	cup grated carrot
3	thinly sliced red bell pepper rings	3	tablespoons chopped green onion
		1/8	teaspoon salt

- Split bagel in half. Spread each half with 2 tablespoons Garden Vegetable Cream Cheese.
- Arrange cucumber and red pepper over cream cheese on bottom half of bagel. Cover with top half of bagel, cream cheese facing vegetables. Cut into quarters. Secure each with a decorative wooden pick.

Garden Vegetable Cream Cheese

- Beat cream cheese in large mixer bowl on high speed 3 minutes or until fluffy, scraping sides of bowl occasionally. Add carrot, green onion and salt. Beat on medium speed 2 minutes or until well-blended, scraping bowl occasionally.

Variation: Neufchatel, light or non-fat cream cheese may be substituted for regular cream cheese.

GRILLED CHICKEN AND BASIL MAYONNAISE BAGEL

Yield: 1 serving

	Basil Mayonnaise	1	ARNIE'S Whole Wheat Bagel, thawed and split
1/3	cup RYKOFF-SEXTON Mayonnaise	1	(5-6 ounce) boneless, skinless TYSON Chicken Breast Half
3	tablespoons chopped fresh basil	1	teaspoon BELLAGIO Olive Oil
			Iceberg lettuce, finely shredded
		2	slices tomato
		2	pieces HORMEL Sliced Bacon, cooked and drained

- To make basil mayonnaise, combine mayonnaise and basil, mixing well.
- Toast bagel in preheated broiler until lightly browned. Spread each half with 1 tablespoon basil mayonnaise; set aside.
- Meanwhile, brush chicken with olive oil. Broil in preheated oven 3-4 minutes per side or until juices are clear when pierced with a fork.
- Spread lettuce over bottom half of bagel. Top with tomatoes. Slice chicken breast horizontally into 4 slices. Place over tomatoes. Top with cooked bacon. Cover with top half of bagel, mayonnaise facing bacon. Serve immediately.

PHILLY PEPPER STEAK

	Sliced green bell pepper	1-2	slices CROSS VALLEY FARMS White American Cheese (optional)
	Sliced onion		
4	ounces RYKOFF-SEXTON Deluxe Beef Chip Steak or QUALITY FOODS Flavored Quality Steak	16" or 7"	hinged sub roll or hoagie roll

- Sauté pepper and onion; set aside. Place 4-ounce portion of steak on flat grill at 325 degrees or moderate to high heat for 1-2 minutes. Turn. After steak has been turned, chip by holding with one spatula and "chipping" with a second spatula. As steak finishes cooking, add sautéed pepper, onion and cheese until it melts.
- Place in roll and serve.

SOUPS & SANDWICHES

MEATS

Polynesian Beef Brochette, page 32

TACO QUESADILLA

Yield: 1 serving

1	OLD EL PASO 10" Flour Tortilla
2	ounces CROSS VALLEY FARMS Pepper Jack Cheese, grated
1	ounce OLD EL PASO Green Chilies, chopped
2	ounces tomato, diced
2	ounces OLD EL PASO Beef Taco Filling, heated
1	ounce iceberg lettuce, shredded
1	ounce sour cream
2	ounces OLD EL PASO Thick 'N Chunky Salsa (medium or mild)

❖ Place the tortilla on a clean, dry grill. Sprinkle cheese, chopped chilies and tomato over the entire tortilla, then top with the hot taco filling.

❖ Fold tortilla in half and cook until the tortilla begins to brown. Turn over and cook until cheese is completely melted and the second side of tortilla begins to brown.

❖ Remove from grill, cut into 4 uniform wedges and place on dinner plate. Garnish with lettuce and sour cream. Serve with a ramekin of salsa on the side.

POLYNESIAN BEEF BROCHETTE

Yield: 25 servings
Serving size: 6 ounces (meat)

12	pounds beef round, cut in 2" cubes
3	cups vinegar
2	cups brown sugar
1/4	cup McCORMICK Curry Powder
1	teaspoon McCORMICK Ground Black Pepper
1	McCORMICK Bay Leaf
1	tablespoon McCORMICK Season-All® Seasoned Salt
1	cup honey
5	green bell peppers, seeded and cut in 2" pieces
5	red bell peppers, seeded and cut in 2" pieces
4	pineapples, fresh, peeled, cored and cut in 2" pieces

❖ Put beef in full-size steam table pans.

❖ Combine next 6 ingredients. Pour over meat. Cover tightly and marinate overnight or up to 3 days.

❖ Remove meat, reserving marinade. Heat marinade to a boil. Stir in honey.

❖ Thread meat on skewers. Broil, brushing frequently with marinade. Cook to desired degree of doneness.

❖ Thread green bell pepper, red bell pepper and pineapple chunks on skewers. Brush with marinade. Broil 5 minutes, brushing twice with marinade.

Taco Quesadilla

Polynesian Beef Brochette

MEATS

SUNDAY DINNER POT ROAST

Yield: 8 servings

1	(3 pound) boneless beef chuck roast, cut 2" thick
2	teaspoons MONTREAL Steak Seasoning
1	cup beef broth
1/2	teaspoon McCORMICK Basil Leaves
1/4	teaspoon McCORMICK Oregano Leaves
1/4	teaspoon McCORMICK Thyme Leaves
4	small potatoes, peeled and halved
4	carrots, cut into 1" pieces
1	medium onion, cut into wedges
	All-purpose flour for thickening (optional)

- Preheat oven to 350 degrees.
- Place meat in 4-quart baking pan and sprinkle with steak seasoning.
- Combine beef broth with basil, oregano and thyme; add to pan.
- Cover and bake in preheated 350-degree oven 1 1/2 hours.
- Uncover meat and scatter potatoes, carrots and onion around roast. Cover and bake 1 1/2 hours or until meat is tender.
- Remove meat from pan and slice. Arrange on serving dish and surround with vegetables. If desired, thicken pan with flour and serve with meat and vegetables.

BEEF STROGANOFF

Yield: 6 servings
Serving size: 1/2 cup

2	tablespoons butter or margarine
1	(2 pound) US FOODSERVICE Beef Tenderloin Steak, cut into bite-sized strips
1/4	cup sherry
1	tablespoon instant minced onion
1	teaspoon McCORMICK Season-All Seasoned Salt
	Dash McCORMICK Ground Nutmeg
1	cup sour cream, room temperature
	Hot cooked wild rice or buttered noodles

- Melt butter in 10" skillet. Add meat and cook 5 minutes, stirring over medium heat.
- Add sherry, minced onion, seasoned salt and nutmeg to skillet and stir. Cover and cook 5 minutes. Remove from heat.
- Stir in sour cream and cook over low heat just until heated through. (Be careful not to let sauce boil. Boiling will make sauce look curdled.)
- Serve over hot cooked wild rice or noodles.

Cooking tip: Beef is easier to slice if partially frozen. Cut across grain into bite-size strips.

CHICKEN FRIED STEAK VERDE

Yield: 1 serving

1	(5.33 ounce or 4 ounce) ADVANCE Chicken Fried Steak
1	slice LA BELLA VILLA Monterey Jack Cheese
	Verde Salsa
	Sour cream

Verde Salsa

	Beef base
1/2	cup water
1/4	teaspoon McCORMICK Garlic Powder
1/4	teaspoon McCORMICK Cayenne Pepper
	Salt
	Pepper
	Cornstarch
1	Hatch Green Chili Pepper, diced
1/4	cup diced onion

- Cook steak according to directions. While still hot, place a slice of Monterey Jack cheese on top of steak. Top with a generous scoop of Verde Salsa and a dollop of sour cream.

Serving suggestion: Serve with Spanish rice and refried beans.

Verde Salsa

- Blend beef base and water in blender (reconstituted to one cup). Add remaining spices and cornstarch to thicken. Finally, mix in chili pepper and diced onion.

BEEF BRISKET

Yield: 18 servings

- $7^1/_2$ pounds US FOODSERVICE Beef Brisket, closely trimmed
- 2 tablespoons salt
- 3 teaspoons McCORMICK Pepper
- 12 ounces onions, minced
- $2^1/_4$ cups CATTLEMEN'S Smoky Barbecue Sauce

❖ *Season brisket with salt, pepper and onion. Place in smoker, fat side up. Smoke $2^1/_2$ hours at 225 degrees. Remove from smoker, place in aluminum foil, fat side down.*

❖ *Pour barbecue sauce over all. Seal foil and place on rack in pan. Bake 3 hours at 250 degrees. Let stand 10 minutes before slicing.*

VEAL PARMIGIANA

Yield: 8 servings
Serving size: 2 cutlets

Sauce

- 1 (6 ounce) can HUNT'S Tomato Paste
- 3/4 cup water
- 1 tablespoon brown sugar
- 1 teaspoon Worcestershire sauce
- 1 teaspoon McCORMICK Season-All Seasoned Salt
- 1/2 teaspoon McCORMICK Italian Seasoning
- 1/4 teaspoon McCORMICK Oregano Leaves
- 1/8 teaspoon McCORMICK Garlic Powder

- 2 eggs
- 1 teaspoon McCORMICK Season-All Seasoned Salt
- 1/4 teaspoon McCORMICK Black Pepper
- 1 cup dry bread crumbs
- 2 pounds RYKOFF-SEXTON Veal Cutlets (16), cut 1/2" thick
- 1/2 cup BELLAGIO Olive Oil
- 1/4 cup grated Parmesan cheese
- 1/2 pound LA BELLA VILLA Mozzarella Cheese, sliced

❖ *Place sauce ingredients in small saucepan and stir to mix. Cook over medium heat, stirring, until slightly thickened. Set aside.*

❖ *Preheat oven to 350 degrees.*

❖ *Place eggs in shallow dish, add seasoned salt and pepper; beat lightly.*

❖ *Place bread crumbs in separate shallow dish or on large piece of wax paper.*

❖ *Dip cutlets into egg mixture and allow excess egg to drip off. Coat on all sides in bread crumbs.*

❖ *Heat oil in large skillet over medium heat and brown cutlets, a few at a time, on both sides.*

❖ *Place cutlets in 13" x 8" x 2" baking pan and pour on reserved sauce. Sprinkle with Parmesan cheese.*

❖ *Cover and bake in preheated 350-degree oven 30 minutes or until meat is tender.*

❖ *Uncover meat and place slices of mozzarella cheese over cutlets. Bake, uncovered, just until cheese melts, about 5 minutes.*

VEAL MARSALA

Yield: 6 servings
Serving size: 2 veal cutlets

- 4 tablespoons butter or margarine, divided
- 2 cups sliced mushrooms
- 2 slices bacon, chopped
- 1/4 cup all-purpose flour
- 1/2 teaspoon McCORMICK Garlic Powder
- 1/2 teaspoon McCORMICK Black Pepper
- $1^1/_2$ pounds RYKOFF-SEXTON Veal Cutlets (12), cut 1/4" thick
- 1 teaspoon cornstarch
- 1/4 cup cold water
- 1/2 cup dry Marsala wine
- 1/2 teaspoon McCORMICK Marjoram Leaves
- 1/4 teaspoon McCORMICK Onion Powder
- 1/4 teaspoon McCORMICK Basil Leaves
- 1/4 teaspoon Bon Appétit

❖ *Melt 1 tablespoon butter in 10" skillet. Add mushrooms and sauté. Remove mushrooms from skillet and set aside.*

❖ *Add chopped bacon to skillet and cook over low heat until cooked, but not crisp. Add 2 tablespoons butter to skillet.*

❖ *Place flour, garlic powder and pepper on plate; stir to combine.*

❖ *Dust veal with flour mixture. Add veal to skillet and sauté, a few pieces at a time, 2 minutes on each side over medium heat. Add remaining 1 tablespoon butter to skillet as needed.*

❖ *Place veal on serving platter and keep warm.*

❖ *Place cornstarch in glass measuring cup. Add water and stir until smooth. Stir in remaining ingredients and pour into skillet.*

❖ *Add reserved mushrooms and cook, stirring over low heat just until mixture begins to boil. Pour over veal. Serve immediately.*

CURE 81® HAM WITH BRANDIED CHERRY GLAZE

Yield: 8-10 servings

1	HORMEL CURE 81® Half Ham
1	(21 ounce) can RYKOFF-SEXTON Cherry Pie Filling
2	tablespoons brandy

❖ Bake ham according to package directions. Thirty minutes before ham is done, spoon pie filling over ham. Continue baking. Just before serving, heat brandy. Pour brandy over ham and ignite.

HAM AND CHEESE STRUDEL WITH MUSTARD SAUCE

Yield: 8 servings

2	cups diced HORMEL CURE 81® Ham
1	cup grated CROSS VALLEY FARMS Swiss Cheese
1	cup sliced fresh mushrooms
1	egg, beaten
1/4	cup chopped green onion
8	frozen phyllo leaves, thawed
1/2	cup melted butter or margarine

Mustard Sauce

1/2	cup sour cream
1/2	cup RYKOFF-SEXTON Mayonnaise or Salad Dressing
2	tablespoons McCORMICK Dry Mustard
1/2	teaspoon sugar

❖ Heat oven to 350 degrees. In bowl, combine ham, cheese, mushrooms, egg and green onion; mix well.
❖ Brush 1 phyllo leaf with butter. Keep remaining leaves covered with a dampened towel to prevent drying.
To assemble, fold leaf in half crosswise; brush with butter. Fold in half crosswise again; brush with butter. Place 1/3 cup ham mixture in center of leaf. Fold long sides up and over filling, overlapping slightly. Fold into thirds from narrow edge.
❖ Place strudel, seam side down, on baking sheet. Cover with dampened towel to prevent drying. Repeat with remaining phyllo leaves, ham mixture and butter. Bake 20 minutes or until golden brown.
❖ To make mustard sauce, combine ingredients in saucepan. Heat over low heat, stirring occasionally, until warm.
❖ Serve strudel with mustard sauce.

Cure 81® Ham with Brandied Cherry Glaze

Ham and Cheese Strudel with Mustard Sauce

MEATS

CREOLE HAM DINNER

Yield: 25 servings
Serving size: 1 cup

15	cups cooked* NEAR EAST Rice
9	cups or 1 #10 can BRYAN Ham Shanks (4 pounds, 5 ounces), drained and chopped
2	cups diced green pepper
2	cups diced onion
3	tablespoons butter
2	tablespoons all-purpose flour
2	tablespoons garlic powder
2	tablespoons McCORMICK Black Pepper
1	#10 can RYKOFF-SEXTON Canned Tomatoes (6 pounds, 6 ounces), with juice

❖ Spray 12" x 20" x 2" steam pan with pan spray and spread rice over bottom. Spread ham shanks over rice. Sauté green pepper and onion in butter until soft. Stir flour, garlic powder and black pepper into onion mixture.

❖ Slowly stir tomatoes into onion mixture and cook until thick. Pour tomato mixture over ham shanks and rice. Bake at 400 degrees for 30 minutes.

*Use drained juices from ham shanks when cooking rice.

PORK MEDALLIONS ST. AUGUSTINE
WITH ZUCCHINI AND SESAME PANCAKES

Yield: 12 servings

3	pounds HORMEL Pork Tenderloin

Marinade

1/2	cup chopped cilantro
1/2	cup sliced green onion
1/2	cup plum wine
1/4	cup vegetable oil
2	jalapeño peppers, seeded and chopped
	Juice of one orange
2	tablespoons balsamic vinegar
2	tablespoons BELLAGIO Olive Oil
1 1/2	tablespoons turmeric
1	tablespoon chopped fresh ginger
1	tablespoon honey
1	tablespoon sesame oil
1	tablespoon soy sauce
6	cloves garlic, crushed
1	teaspoon McCORMICK Cumin
1/2	teaspoon McCORMICK White Pepper

Sauce

	Reserved marinade
1	cup toasted cashews
1/2	cup plum wine
1 1/2	cups RYKOFF-SEXTON Ham Stock

Zucchini and Sesame Pancakes

2	medium zucchinis
1 1/2-2	cups all-purpose flour
2	eggs
1/4	cup sesame seeds, toasted
2	tablespoons chopped fresh ginger
2	tablespoons chopped onion
2	tablespoons soy sauce
	Nutmeg
	Salt
	Pepper

❖ Clean and cut pork tenderloin into medallions.

❖ Combine all marinade ingredients. Marinate pork for 6 hours. Remove from marinade and pat dry. Reserve marinade. Sear pork medallions on both sides until brown. Finish in oven at 375 degrees 8-10 minutes.

❖ To make sauce, place reserved marinade and cashews into food processor. Process until smooth. In a saucepan, reduce wine by half. Add a small amount of pureed marinade and de-glaze until brown. Add ham stock and remaining pureed marinade. Cook until desired consistency.

Serving suggestions: Serve with a chilled seasonal melon salad garnished with orange zest and mint. If desired, couscous and sautéed zucchini slices can be substituted.

Zucchini and Sesame Pancakes

❖ Grate zucchinis and combine with remaining ingredients. Heat pan with oil. Add tablespoon-sized dollops of batter. Spread and cook until brown on both sides. Reserve. Reheat when ready to serve. Serve with pork medallions.

MEATS

CARIBBEAN LIME-GRILLED PORK

Yield: 12 servings

12   (6 ounce) HORMEL Pork Sirloin Roast Chops, ¾" thick

Marinade
- 3 cups fresh lime juice
- 2 teaspoons salt
- 1 teaspoon crushed McCORMICK Red Pepper
- 1 teaspoon McCORMICK Cayenne
- 2 large red onions

❖ Place pork chops in glass or enamel pan. Combine lime juice, salt, crushed red pepper and cayenne. Pour over pork.
❖ Cut onions into ¼" thick slices and place on top of pork. Spoon lime juice over onions to coat. Cover and refrigerate at least 6 hours.
❖ Remove pork from marinade, reserving onions and marinade. Grill pork chops until desired doneness or maximum internal temperature of 160 degrees.
❖ Place reserved onion slices and marinade in saucepan. Simmer 14 minutes.

Serving suggestion: Serve pork with cooked red onions and fruited coconut rice.

GLAZED PORK ROLLATINI

Yield: 12 servings

Mustard Cream
- 1 tablespoon minced onion
- 1 tablespoon butter
- 1 cup cream
- ½ cup GREY POUPON® Dijon Mustard
- Salt
- Pepper
- 3 pounds boneless HORMEL Pork Loin

Mushroom Stuffing
- 3 garlic cloves, crushed
- 1 onion, chopped
- 1 pound portobello mushrooms, sliced
- 8 ounces butter
- ½ pound sun-dried tomatoes, chopped
- 1 pound fresh mozzarella, diced
- 1½ cups fresh watercress sprigs

Cooked pasta

❖ To prepare mustard cream sauce, sauté onion in butter; stir in cream, mustard and salt and pepper to taste. Simmer gently to heat through. Keep warm.
❖ Butterfly pork loin, lay flat, butterfly again, lay flat and pound out to approximately 12" x 18," about ¼" thick.
❖ To make stuffing, in large skillet, sauté garlic, onion and mushrooms in butter until limp. Cook and stir to evaporate liquid given off by mushrooms. Quickly stir in tomatoes and cheese to a smooth paste.
❖ Spread mushroom stuffing evenly over pork, top with watercress, roll up and tie evenly. Roast in a 350-degree oven for 20-25 minutes, until browned and cooked through. Let sit 10 minutes before slicing.
❖ Serve 2 slices rollatini per serving, mapped with mustard cream and accompanied with pasta.

Caribbean Lime-Grilled Pork

Glazed Pork Rollatini

MEATS

PORK FILET MIGNON

Yield: 12 servings

<u>Roasted Shallot Jus</u> (yield 1/2 pints)
3	quarts pork or veal stock
6	shallots, sliced
2	tablespoons BELLAGIO Olive Oil
	Salt
	White pepper

24	(2 ounce) HORMEL Pork Tenderloin Medallions
	Salt
	Pepper
	Olive oil

- To make jus, reduce stock by 2/3; set aside. In a 350-degree oven, roast shallots in oil in shallow pan for 1 hour or until soft. Puree shallots and whisk into reduced stock; season with salt and pepper. Strain and keep warm to serve.
- Season pork medallions with salt and pepper, brush with olive oil and grill on hot griddle 2-3 minutes per side, until medium.

BOURBON BARBECUE GLAZED PORK CUTLETS

Yield: 12 servings

<u>Bourbon Brine</u>
6	cups Kentucky bourbon
2	pounds carrots, peeled and chopped
2	pounds onion, peeled and chopped
1	pound celery, chopped
1/2	cup juniper berries
1	garlic clove head, crushed
3	McCORMICK Cinnamon Sticks
8	bay leaves
2	pounds brown sugar
2	cups kosher salt
1/2	cup black peppercorns
1	gallon water
1	(6 pound) boneless HORMEL Pork Loin, trimmed

<u>Barbecue Glaze</u>
3	cups light corn syrup
1	cup molasses
1	cup HEINZ Ketchup
2	teaspoons McCORMICK Cayenne
1/2	teaspoon McCORMICK Ground Cloves
1/2	teaspoon McCORMICK Ground Cinnamon
1/2	teaspoon McCORMICK Ground Allspice
3	tablespoons McCORMICK Chopped Garlic
3	tablespoons McCORMICK Chopped Onion
1	cup Worcestershire sauce
2	cups vegetable oil
3	tablespoons hot pepper sauce
1	ounce Kentucky bourbon
	Chopped tomato
	Fresh sage

- In a large stockpot, bring to a boil all brine ingredients. Reduce heat and simmer 30 minutes. Chill before adding pork loin.
- Mix all barbecue glaze ingredients well and set aside.
- Soak loin in bourbon brine; refrigerate for 48 hours. Remove loin from brine, pat dry and cut into 36 (2 ounce) cutlets; pound to 1/8" thick. Dip cutlets into barbecue glaze; sear on hot grill 1 minute on both sides, making cross-hatch pattern on both sides. Place on rack under broiler and broil on 1 side about 3 minutes. Dip in glaze again and broil on other side 3 minutes or until internal temperature reaches 140 degrees. Dip cutlets in barbecue glaze once more before putting on plate.
- To serve, plate 3 cutlets, garnishing with chopped tomato and a sprig of fresh sage.

Serving suggestions: Serve with apple-bread stuffing and whipped sweet potatoes or roasted onions.

SAVORY POT PIE

3	pounds beef, pork or turkey, cooked
3 1/2	pounds PILLSBURY Seasoned Idaho® Potato Bursts™, prepared
1	cup bread crumbs
1	quart brown gravy
1	cup sautéed onion, finely diced
2	tablespoons minced garlic
1	teaspoon ground allspice

1	teaspoon black pepper
2	(12 ounce) PILLSBURY Puff Pastry Sheets, 10" x 15" (1 per pan as bottom crust)
2	(12 ounce) PILLSBURY Puff Pastry Sheets, 10" x 15" (1 per pan as top crust)
	Egg wash (1 part egg, 1 part water)
2	quarts brown gravy (optional)

- Mix meat and potatoes together.
- Add bread crumbs, gravy, onion, garlic, allspice and pepper to meat/potato mixture. Set aside.
- Roll puff pastry to fit bottom and sides of half steam table pan; dock.
- Add meat filling to crust-lined half steam table pans.
- Roll two remaining puff pastry sheets to fit as top crust for the 2 half pans.
- Press edges together.
- Vent crusts and brush on egg wash as needed.
- Bake at 375 degrees in a conventional oven (325 degrees in a convection oven) about 50 minutes or until crust is a rich golden brown.
- To serve: cut each pan in 2" x 6." Serve 1 portion with 2 ounces brown gravy, if desired.

MEATS

Wood Grilled and Barbecued Double Thick Chops

Savory Pot Pie

WOOD GRILLED AND BARBECUED DOUBLE THICK CHOPS

Yield: 12 servings

<u>Brining Solution</u>
2	gallons water
2	cups (1 1/2 pounds) honey
2	cups kosher salt
4	heads garlic, cut in half
2	tablespoons black peppercorns
8	bay leaves
2	pieces HORMEL Pork Loin (10-12 pounds), trimmed

<u>Bourbon Molasses Barbecue Sauce</u>
2	Spanish onions, diced
2	Granny Smith apples, diced
1/4	cup RYKOFF-SEXTON Canola Oil
3	cups HEINZ Ketchup
1	cup HEINZ Red Wine Vinegar
1/2	cup bourbon
1/4	cup molasses
1/4	cup dry mustard powder
2	tablespoons chopped fresh rosemary
1	tablespoon McCORMICK Cayenne Pepper

<u>Fire-Roasted Salsa</u>
1	Spanish onion, diced
5	cloves garlic, peeled and halved
4	jalapeño peppers, seeded and diced
8	plum tomatoes, cored
2	tablespoons BELLAGIO Olive Oil
1	cup water
1/4	cup fresh lime juice
1	bunch chopped fresh cilantro
2	Ancho chili peppers, seeded
2	teaspoons McCORMICK Ground Cumin
	Salt
	Pepper

- ❖ Combine all Brining Solution ingredients. Submerge pork in mixture for 3 hours.
- ❖ To prepare barbecue sauce, sauté onions and apples in oil in large pot until slightly caramelized. Add remaining sauce ingredients and simmer for 1 hour. Strain and cool before using.
- ❖ For salsa: Spread onion, garlic and jalapeños in heavy pan. Cover with tomatoes and drizzle with oil. Cook mixture under broiler until tomatoes are well-charred. Cool to room temperature. Place mixture in blender or food processor. Add water, lime juice, cilantro, Ancho chilies and cumin. Blend until well-combined but not completely liquified. Season with salt and pepper.
- ❖ Roast loin on rotisserie or in 350-degree oven about 45-60 minutes until medium or internal temperature is approximately 155 degrees. Let sit 10 minutes, then cut into double thick chops. Finish chops over wood grill or barbecue, continually basting with sauce until well-glazed.

Serving suggestion: Serve pork chops with warm salsa and jalapeño-Cheddar cornbread.

MEATS

Pesto Stuffed Pork with Plum Sauce

PESTO STUFFED PORK WITH PLUM SAUCE
Yield: 12 servings

24   (2 ounce) HORMEL Pork Loin Chops

Marinade
6	cups teriyaki sauce
1/2	cup julienned ginger root
8	large cloves garlic, minced
1/4	cup Szechwan peppercorns
16	star anise, crushed

Oriental Pesto
3	cups chopped cilantro
2	cups grated Parmesan cheese
1/2	cup pine nuts, toasted
1/2	cup chopped tarragon
2	jalapeños, roasted, peeled and seeded
3	tablespoons McCORMICK Grated Ginger
6	cloves garlic, crushed

    Salt
    Pepper
1 1/4	cups olive oil
2	tablespoons sesame oil
1/2	cup sesame seeds, toasted

Sweet and Sour Plum Sauce
10	plums, pitted and halved
1	cup RYKOFF-SEXTON Apple Cider Vinegar
1	cup packed brown sugar
1	cup port wine
3/4	cup raspberry vinegar
1/2	cup red currant jelly
2	tablespoons RYKOFF-SEXTON Lemon Juice
1 1/2	teaspoons grated fresh ginger
1 1/2	teaspoons salt
1/4	teaspoon McCORMICK Ground Clove

❖ Cut a pocket into side of each chop. Combine all marinade ingredients together. Marinate chops for 2-3 hours turning occasionally.
❖ Combine all pesto ingredients in a food processor, except for the oils and toasted sesame seeds. Add oils gradually, pulsing repeatedly to incorporate. Add sesame seeds just before stuffing chops.
❖ In a saucepan, simmer plum sauce ingredients until plums are tender, about 25-30 minutes. Puree in a food processor. Remove pork from marinade.
❖ Fill pockets of each chop with pesto. Char-grill pork chops until done.
❖ Serve with plum sauce. Garnish as desired.

SAUSAGE CASSEROLE
Yield: 6-8 servings

1	(10 ounce) box long grain and wild rice
1	pound JIMMY DEAN® Brick Sausage, cooked, crumbled and drained
1	(10 3/4 ounce) can cream of mushroom soup
1/2	cup evaporated milk
1/2	onion, chopped

❖ Prepare rice according to directions on box. Add sausage and other ingredients; mix well. Bake in 350-degree oven for 30 minutes.

MEATS

SAUSAGE AND POTATO PIE

Yield: 12 servings

3	cups corn flakes, crushed to 1 1/2 cups	1	pound JIMMY DEAN® Brick Sausage
1/4	cup finely chopped onion	2	eggs
1/2	teaspoon salt	2	cups thawed LAMB-WESTON Loose-Pack Hash Brown Potatoes
1/4	teaspoon McCORMICK Pepper		
1/4	teaspoon McCORMICK Garlic Powder	1	tablespoon melted butter
1	tablespoon McCORMICK Prepared Mustard	1/2	cup grated CROSS VALLEY FARMS Cheddar Cheese
1/3	cup milk		

❖ Combine 1 cup corn flakes, onion, salt, pepper, garlic powder, mustard and milk; mix well. Add sausage, stirring until combined. Press mixture evenly in bottom of 9" x 9" baking pan.

❖ In small bowl, beat eggs slightly. Add hash brown potatoes to eggs; mix well. Spread mixture evenly over meat. Bake at 350 degrees for 35 minutes. Combine remaining corn flakes with melted butter; set aside. Remove dish from oven.

❖ Sprinkle cheese evenly over top; add corn flake mixture. Return to oven for 10 more minutes until cheese melts.

SAUSAGE FAJITAS

Yield: 6-8 servings

1	red bell pepper, sliced
1	green bell pepper, sliced
1	onion, sliced
1	pound JIMMY DEAN® Brick Sausage, sliced into 1/2" strips, cooked and drained
1	(10 count) package flour tortillas
	CROSS VALLEY FARMS Cheddar Cheese, grated
	PACE Picante Sauce
	Sour cream

❖ Sauté peppers and onion in small amount of sausage drippings. Warm tortillas and fill with sausage, peppers, onion and cheese. Serve with Cheddar cheese, picante sauce and sour cream.

HOLIDAY LOIN ROAST WITH SUN-DRIED FRUITS

Yield: 24 servings

1	(8 pound) boneless HORMEL Pork Loin		*Chive-and-Corn-Studded Mashed Potatoes*
		6	pounds potatoes, peeled and chopped
Stuffing			Salted water
1	medium red onion, finely chopped	6	ears fresh corn
1/2	cup BELLAGIO Olive Oil	1/4	cup olive oil
2	cups chopped dried apricots	4	cups milk
2	cups dried cranberries	1	bunch chives, snipped
2	cups black raisins		Salt
2	cups golden raisins		Cayenne pepper
1	bunch fresh sage, chopped		
	Salt		*Sautéed Swiss Chard*
	Pepper	6	bunches red Swiss chard
	Chive-and-Corn-Studded Mashed Potatoes	1/4	cup olive oil
	Sautéed Swiss Chard		

❖ Force a steel through face of loin to create tunnel for stuffing.

❖ Cook onion in olive oil until translucent. Add dried fruits, sage, salt and pepper. Cover with lid. Let cool so fruit will plump. Fill piping bag with mixture and force stuffing into loin. Sear loin to a golden brown and roast in a 350-degree oven to medium doneness, 150-160 degrees, about 1 1/2 hours.

❖ Slice and serve with Chive-and-Corn-Studded Mashed Potatoes and Sautéed Swiss Chard.

Chive-and-Corn-Studded Mashed Potatoes

❖ Cook potatoes in salted water. Strip ears of corn and sauté in oil. In mixing bowl, add potatoes and milk. Mash and add corn. Finish with chives and salt and pepper to taste.

Sautéed Swiss Chard

❖ Wash, dry and chop chard. Sauté in oil.

MEATS

Holiday Loin Roast with Sun-Dried Fruits

Truffled Pork Ragout

TRUFFLED PORK RAGOUT

Yield: 10 servings
Serving size: 1 1/2 cups

4	pounds boneless HORMEL Pork Loin
1/4	cup vegetable oil
8	garlic cloves, crushed
1	tablespoon chopped fresh thyme
1	tablespoon McCORMICK Black Peppercorns
1	tablespoon Szechwan peppercorns
1	tablespoon salt
1/8	teaspoon ground cloves
1	teaspoon McCORMICK Ground Cumin
1	teaspoon chili paste (with garlic)
1	tablespoon palm sugar or brown sugar
1	tablespoon tamarind paste or lemon juice
1	quart pork stock
28	ounces sparkling cider
1/2	cup Riesling or fruity white wine
3	tablespoons cornstarch
1-2	ounces truffle pieces
2	tablespoons sugar
4	tablespoons butter
3	large Rome Beauty apples, cored and wedged
1	cup corn kernels
1	cup sliced zucchini (1/2")
1	cup sliced chanterelle mushrooms

❖ Dice pork loin.
❖ Heat oil in large braising pot. Combine garlic, thyme, black peppercorns, Szechwan peppercorns, salt, cloves and cumin. Toss well with pork cubes. Brown seasoned pork, in batches, if necessary. Add chili paste, brown sugar, tamarind paste or lemon juice, stock and cider to pan. Cover and simmer 30-40 minutes.
❖ Combine wine and cornstarch. Stir into ragout and return to a boil. Cook 5-8 minutes, stirring. Remove from heat, stir in truffles, cover and let stand 30 minutes. Sauce should be syrupy, not thick.
❖ Heat sugar and 2 tablespoons butter together in large sauté pan. When mixture begins to caramelize, add apples and sauté until golden. Remove from heat and keep warm.
❖ Steam corn and zucchini until tender. Sauté mushrooms in 2 tablespoons butter.
❖ Ladle ragout onto serving plates. Garnish with corn, zucchini, mushrooms and apples.

Serving suggestion: Serve with mashed potatoes.

MEATS

SEAFOOD

Maryland-Style Crab Cakes, page 50

Shrimp Creole Port au Prince

Saucy Shrimp Kabobs

SHRIMP CREOLE PORT AU PRINCE

Yield: 24 servings
Serving size: 4 ounces shrimp (plus sauce and rice)

1	cup olive oil	1/3	cup McCORMICK Caribbean Jerk Seasoning
16	garlic cloves, finely chopped	8	cups RYKOFF-SEXTON Tomato Sauce
4	medium onions, finely chopped	4	cups beer
4	large green bell peppers, finely chopped	6	pounds raw BEE GEE Shrimp, (P&D, $^{41}/_{50}$ count), tails cut off
4	OLD EL PASO Jalapeño Peppers, finely chopped		Salt
1	cup chopped fresh parsley, divided		Cooked rice
4	McCORMICK Bay Leaves	1	(14 ounce) jar red bell peppers, roasted and sliced or pimento, sliced
4	teaspoons McCORMICK Oregano		

- ❖ Heat olive oil in a large, deep skillet. Sauté garlic, onions, green peppers, jalapeño peppers, 3 tablespoons parsley, bay leaves, oregano and Caribbean Jerk Seasoning. Cook 3 minutes.
- ❖ Add tomato sauce and beer. Simmer over medium heat for 10 minutes or until sauce thickens slightly.
- ❖ Add shrimp; cook 4 minutes. Add salt, if necessary.
- ❖ Serve hot in a casserole with cooked rice. Garnish with remaining parsley and roasted pepper strips.

SAUCY SHRIMP KABOBS

Yield: 19 skewers

3½	pounds BEE GEE Shrimp (13-15 count), peeled and deveined
1	pound, 12 ounces red onion, cut in large pieces
1	pound small whole mushrooms
3½	cups sliced crookneck squash (½")
2	cups green bell pepper pieces (1")
2	cups red bell pepper pieces (1")
2	pounds, 6 ounces HUNT'S OPEN RANGE® Original or Hickory Flavor Barbecue Sauce

- ❖ On each skewer, alternately thread shrimp and vegetables.
- ❖ Place skewers on sheet pan.
- ❖ Evenly spread barbecue sauce over skewers, turning to coat both sides.
- ❖ Broil until shrimp is pink and vegetables are tender, turning once.

SEAFOOD

SHRIMP SALAD NIÇOISE

Yield: 12 servings

2 1/4	pounds ICELANDIC® Brand Shrimp (250-350 count)		Lettuce
1 1/2	cups RYKOFF-SEXTON Vinaigrette (or your favorite mild vinegar & oil dressing)	6	hard boiled PAPETTI'S Eggs, cut in eighths
		48	medium pitted olives
3	pounds RYKOFF-SEXTON Cooked Potatoes, sliced or diced	12	anchovy fillets (optional)
		6	tomatoes, cut in sixths
3	pounds RYKOFF-SEXTON Cooked Green Beans		

❖ Just before serving, toss shrimp with 2 tablespoons dressing; set aside. Combine potatoes with 2 tablespoons dressing; set aside. Season green beans and tomatoes with 2 tablespoons dressing; set aside.

❖ Line plates with beds of lettuce. Arrange potatoes, green beans, tomatoes, eggs and olives (and anchovy fillets, if desired) attractively on plates. In the center of each plate, place a mound of shrimp. Spoon remaining dressing over salad.

SHRIMP FRA DIAVOLO

Yield: 8 1/2 pounds sauce

1/2	cup minced garlic	1/2	cup oregano leaves
1	cup olive oil	2	cups dry white wine
2	quarts PACE® Thick & Chunky Salsa	1 1/2	pounds medium BEE GEE Shrimp
2	quarts water	1	cup chopped fresh parsley
6	pounds tomato, chopped	6	pounds SAN GIORGIO Linguini, cooked

❖ In skillet, sauté garlic in oil.
❖ Add salsa, water, tomato and oregano leaves to sautéed garlic and bring to boil. Simmer for 10 minutes.
❖ Add white wine and simmer 10 more minutes.
❖ Peel and devein shrimp. Add to skillet along with parsley and simmer 3 minutes.
❖ Serve sauce over pasta.

SHRIMP QUESADILLAS

Yield: 2 servings

2	tablespoons olive oil	2	large flour tortillas
1	red or yellow bell pepper, julienned	1	cup grated CROSS VALLEY FARMS Monterey Jack Cheese
1	small onion, julienned		Sour cream
8	ounces BEE GEE Cooked Shrimp		Guacamole
4	ripe plum tomatoes, peeled and diced 1/4"		Salsa

❖ Heat oil in medium skillet; sauté pepper and onion. Add shrimp just long enough to heat. Then add tomatoes and toss. Arrange tortillas in the traditional manner. Garnish with cheese, sour cream, guacamole and salsa.

Serving suggestion: Serve with your favorite rice and beans.

CURRIED SHRIMP ROLLERS

Yield: 24 servings
Serving size: 1 sandwich

3	pounds ICELANDIC® Brand Shrimp, defrosted and drained well		Curry Sauce
		1	quart diced apple pieces
2	quarts Curry Sauce	3	cups RYKOFF-SEXTON Light Mayonnaise
24	soft lavash or mountain bread, 8" diameter	1 1/2	ounces scallions, minced
24	lettuce leaves	1 1/2	cups dark seedless raisins
		3	tablespoons McCORMICK Curry Powder

❖ In bowl, combine shrimp and curry sauce; mix well.
❖ For each sandwich, line an 8" lavash with lettuce leaf. Top with 1/2 cup shrimp salad mixture and roll up sandwich. Cut rolled sandwich diagonally to serve.

Note: This recipe works equally well with ICELANDIC® Brand Scallops.

Curry Sauce
❖ In bowl, combine all ingredients; mix well. Cover and refrigerate at least 2 hours.

SEAFOOD

STADIUM SHRIMP IN BEER

Yield: 6 servings

2	large garlic cloves, minced	2	tablespoons minced shallots or green onion
1/2	teaspoon salt	2	tablespoons tarragon or red wine vinegar
1	(12 ounce) bottle beer	1	tablespoon Dijon mustard
1/2-1	teaspoon McCORMICK Crushed Red Pepper Flakes	1	tablespoon grainy mustard
1/4	teaspoon McCORMICK White Pepper	2	tablespoons olive oil
1	pound medium or large shrimp (in shell)	1	tablespoon minced fresh tarragon or parsley

- In medium saucepan, stir together garlic, salt, beer, red pepper flakes and white pepper. Cover, bring to boil and simmer 3 minutes.
- Stir in shrimp and quickly bring to a boil. Reduce heat to low, cover and simmer for 2 minutes. Pour shrimp and liquid into a heat-proof glass or ceramic bowl and cover lightly with plastic wrap. Refrigerate 1 hour or overnight.
- Remove shrimp with a slotted spoon and pour liquid into a medium saucepan. Bring to a boil and continue boiling uncovered until reduced to 1/4 cup, approximately 6-8 minutes. Remove from heat and whisk in shallots, vinegar, Dijon mustard, grainy mustard and oil. Pour sauce over shrimp. Cover and marinate. Make shrimp up to 2 days in advance, if desired. Stir in tarragon or parsley before serving.

CERDO CAMARONERO (PORK AND SHRIMP)

Yield: 12 servings

18	HORMEL Bacon Strips (1 pound)	*Salsa*	
1	pound medium shrimp (36 count)	2	red bell peppers, seeded and finely diced
5	pieces pork tenderloin, trimmed, flattened slightly and sliced into 1" medallions (4 1/2-5 pounds)	1	avocado, peeled, pitted and diced
3/4	cup ground achiote paste	1	bunch cilantro, minced
1	cup BELLAGIO Olive Oil	2	avocados, peeled, pitted and sliced

Lemon Butter Sauce
1	cup beef stock (bouillon or demi-glace)
	Juice of 4 lemons
	Juice of 4 limes
2	cups butter
	Salt
	Pepper

- Cut bacon strips in half. Wrap each shrimp with bacon strip, securing bacon with toothpicks to form mini-skewers. Place skewers in sauté pan or on grill and cook until shrimp are cooked through and bacon is crispy, about 3-5 minutes.
- Rub pork slices with achiote paste. Heat oil in sauté pan over high heat. Add pork slices and cook 5 minutes. Turn pork and cook 3 minutes on other side or until desired doneness.
- For sauce: Reduce beef stock, lemon juice and lime juice in pan by 1/3. Whisk in butter until melted and smooth. Season with salt and pepper.
- For salsa: Combine bell peppers, diced avocado and cilantro.
- To serve, place pork and shrimp on plate. Pour sauce over pork. Serve with avocado and red pepper salsa and garnish with avocado slices.

BLACK FOREST SEAGRILL

Yield: 24 servings
Serving size: 1 sandwich

24	slices black bread	*Hot Cabbage Kraut*	
3	cups RYKOFF-SEXTON Lowfat Thousand Island Dressing	3	tablespoons BELLAGIO Olive Oil
1 1/2	quarts *Hot Cabbage Kraut*	2 1/2	pounds red cabbage, sliced
24	(5 ounce) ICELANDIC® Brand SeaGrills®, cooked according to package directions	1 1/4	pounds red onion, thinly sliced
		1	cup white vinegar
24	(1 ounce) slices lowfat Swiss cheese (1 1/2 pounds)	1/4	cup brown sugar
		1	teaspoon salt
		1/2	teaspoon McCORMICK Ground Black Pepper

- For each sandwich, spread a slice of bread with 2 tablespoons dressing.
- Spread 1/4 cup Hot Cabbage Kraut over dressing and top with prepared fish.
- Lay slice of cheese over fish, and bake at 400 degrees until sandwich is hot and cheese is melted.

Note: This recipe works equally well with all ICELANDIC® Brand fillet portions.

Hot Cabbage Kraut
- In large skillet, heat oil; add cabbage and onion, and cook for 5 minutes, stirring often.
- Add vinegar, sugar, salt and pepper, and continue cooking 20 minutes or until liquid is evaporated and kraut is tender.

SEAFOOD

CLAM RATATOUILLE

Yield: 10 servings
Serving size: 8 ounces

Cooking method: Braising/Sautéing

2	tablespoons BELLAGIO Olive Oil	1	pound yellow squash, diced
1	pound onion, diced	1	pound green beans, diced
1	pound scallions, diced	1	pound eggplant, diced
2	tablespoons minced garlic	16	ounces canned EASTERN SHORE Clam Juice
1	pound green bell pepper, diced	80	ounces canned EASTERN SHORE Chopped Clams
1	pound red bell pepper, diced	1	teaspoon McCORMICK Oregano
1	pound yellow bell pepper, diced	1	teaspoon McCORMICK Thyme
1	pound zucchini, diced	1	teaspoon McCORMICK Basil
		1	pound tomatoes, diced
		6	ounces Parmesan cheese, grated

- ❖ Heat oil in heavy pan. Add all the vegetables except tomatoes. Add clam juice and cook down for about 15 minutes. Then, add chopped clams and Italian seasonings. Continue to cook for about 5 more minutes.
- ❖ Garnish with diced tomatoes and grated Parmesan cheese.

Serving suggestion: Serve over buttered pasta or as a clam casserole.

CLAM ENCHILADAS

Yield: 2 servings
Serving size: 4 ounces

Cooking method: Sautéing/Baking

1	tablespoon BELLAGIO Olive Oil	2	flour tortillas
3	ounces onion, finely diced	4	ounces CROSS VALLEY FARMS Cheddar Cheese, grated
3	ounces scallions, finely diced	4	ounces Monterey Jack cheese, grated
1	teaspoon minced garlic		Salt
2	ounces red bell pepper, finely diced		Pepper
2	ounces green bell pepper, finely diced		
2	ounces green onion, finely diced		*Garnish*
1	(6 ounce) can EASTERN SHORE Chopped Clams, drained	2	ounces romaine lettuce, shredded
2	teaspoons finely diced cilantro	4	ounces tomato, diced
1	teaspoon McCORMICK Oregano	2	ounces sour cream
		4	black olives, thinly sliced

- ❖ Heat olive oil in pot, cook onion, scallions, garlic, red bell pepper, green bell pepper and green onion until tender and translucent. Add chopped clams and cook for 5-7 minutes over medium heat. Add cilantro and remaining seasonings. Cook mixture for another 3 minutes. Turn off stove and let sit.
- ❖ Heat flour tortillas on grill or over direct flame until warm. Stuff each tortilla with 3 ounces of clam mixture and about 1 ounce of cheeses, then fold or roll. Arrange on dinner plate and return to hot oven just long enough to melt cheese.
- ❖ Top with shredded lettuce, tomato, sour cream and black olives.

Variation: For spicier recipe, add fresh jalapeños or crushed red pepper seasoning to the vegetables while they cook.

Clam Ratatouille

Clam Enchiladas

SEAFOOD

CLAM TACOS

Cooking method: Sautéing/Baking

Yield: 2 servings
Serving size: 4 ounces

1	tablespoon BELLAGIO Olive Oil
3	ounces onion, finely diced
3	ounces scallions, finely diced
1	teaspoon minced garlic
2	ounces red bell pepper, finely diced
2	ounces green bell pepper, finely diced
2	ounces green onion, finely diced
1	(6 ounce) can EASTERN SHORE Chopped Clams, drained
2	teaspoons finely diced cilantro
1	teaspoon McCORMICK Oregano
2	taco shells

- 4 ounces CROSS VALLEY FARMS Cheddar Cheese, grated
- 4 ounces CROSS VALLEY FARMS Monterey Jack Cheese, grated
- Salt
- Black pepper

Garnish
- 2 ounces romaine lettuce, shredded
- 4 ounces tomato, diced
- 2 ounces sour cream
- 4 black olives, thinly sliced

❖ Heat olive oil in pot, cook onion, scallions, garlic, red bell pepper, green bell pepper and green onion until tender and translucent. Add chopped clams and cook for 5-7 minutes over medium heat. Add cilantro and remaining seasonings. Cook mixture for another 3 minutes. Turn off stove and let sit.

❖ Heat taco shells in oven for about 1 minute. Stuff each taco with 3 ounces of clam mixture and top with about 1 ounce cheeses. Arrange on dinner plate and return to hot oven just long enough to melt cheese.

❖ Top with shredded lettuce, tomato, sour cream and black olives.

Variation: For spicier recipe, add fresh jalapeños or crushed red pepper seasoning to the vegetables while they cook.

BROILED SALMON STEAKS WITH DILL SAUCE

Yield: 4 servings

- 1 tablespoon margarine
- 1/4 cup dry white wine
- 1 tablespoon finely chopped fresh parsley
- 1/4 teaspoon dried dill
- 1 clove garlic, minced
- 1 pound pink salmon steaks or fillets

❖ In small saucepan, combine margarine, wine, parsley, dill and garlic. Heat slowly until margarine is melted. Rinse salmon under cold water. Pat dry. Place fish on broiler pan and brush with sauce.

❖ Cook for 9 minutes per inch thickness, turning halfway through estimated cooking time. Baste with sauce when turning. Fish is done when meat is just opaque throughout and flakes easily when tested with a fork.

Variations: May use other fish fillets or steak of choice.

LOWFAT FIESTA FISH TACOS

- 2 OLD EL PASO 6" Flour Tortillas
- 1 ounce Green Chili Mayonnaise
- 2 (2 ounce) unbreaded ARCTIC HARVEST Fish Fillets (no oil or butter added)
- 2 ounces green and red cabbage mix, shredded
- 1 ounce OLD EL PASO Thick N' Chunky Salsa (mild or medium)
- 1/2 ounce reduced-fat Cheddar cheese, grated
- Salsa (additional)

Green Chili Mayonnaise   Yield: 4 quarts
- 2 quarts reduced-fat mayonnaise
- 1 cup OLD EL PASO Picante Sauce (medium or mild)
- 1 (27 ounce) can OLD EL PASO Green Chilies, chopped

❖ Heat tortillas on grill or in microwave, and place on counter. Spread each tortilla with Green Chili Mayonnaise and top with fish fillet.

❖ Toss cabbage mix with salsa and place 1 ounce on top of each fish fillet. Sprinkle with grated cheese and place on a dinner plate. Serve with a ramekin of salsa on the side.

Green Chili Mayonnaise

❖ Combine all ingredients together, place in storage container, cover, date and refrigerate until needed.

SEAFOOD

PAN-ASIAN COUNTRY FRY

Yield: 24 servings
Serving size: 1 sandwich

24	(3 1/4 ounce) ICELANDIC® Brand Country Fry
48	*Scallion Pancakes*
3	cups *Hoisin Mayonnaise*
1	quart *Oriental Slaw*
24	medium radishes, grated
1 1/2	tablespoons sesame seeds, toasted

Scallion Pancakes

1 1/2	cups water, boiling
2 1/2	pounds all-purpose flour
1 1/2	teaspoons salt
2	tablespoons vegetable oil
2	cups thinly sliced scallions
	Vegetable oil

Hoisin Mayonnaise

2	cups light mayonnaise
1	cup Hoisin sauce (Chinese BBQ sauce)
1/2	cup minced scallions

Oriental Slaw

1/4	cup rice vinegar
1	teaspoon minced garlic
1/2	teaspoon salt
1/2	teaspoon hot red pepper sauce
1 1/4	pounds green cabbage, finely shredded
1	cup finely grated carrot
1	cup finely sliced onion
1 1/2	tablespoons dark sesame oil
1 1/2	tablespoons vegetable oil

- ❖ For each sandwich, on one Scallion Pancake spread 2 tablespoons Hoisin Mayonnaise.
- ❖ Top with 3 tablespoons Oriental Slaw. Place prepared crisp country fry on slaw. Sprinkle with 2 tablespoons grated radish and approximately 1/2 teaspoon sesame seeds. Top with second Scallion Pancake and serve hot.

Scallion Pancakes
- ❖ In large bowl, stir water into flour and salt mixture to make very soft dough. Knead until smooth. Let sit 30 minutes.
- ❖ Cut dough into 6 pieces and roll each into 12" x 7" rectangles. Brush with oil and sprinkle with scallions. Roll each rectangle into a log, starting with long side. Cut each into 8 pieces and roll out each piece into 4 1/2" rounds.
- ❖ Cook in lightly oiled skillet over high heat until crisp and browned on both sides.

Hoisin Mayonnaise
- ❖ In bowl, combine all ingredients; cover and refrigerate at least 2 hours.

Oriental Slaw
- ❖ In bowl, combine all ingredients; drizzle with oil and toss. Let stand 2 hours before serving.

Lowfat Fiesta Fish Tacos

Pan-Asian Country Fry

SEAFOOD

Maryland-Style Crab Cakes

Grilled Salmon with Dijon-Maple Ginger Basting Sauce

MARYLAND-STYLE CRAB CAKES

Yield: 6 servings
Serving size: 9 ounces

Sauce
1 1/2	cups pureed roasted peppers
2	tablespoons finely chopped shallots
1	teaspoon minced garlic
2	tablespoons BELLAGIO Balsamic Vinegar
1	teaspoon sugar

1/2	cup cornmeal
2 1/3	cups bread crumbs, divided
1 1/4	pounds crabmeat, drained
1	cup FLEISCHMANN'S® Egg Beaters® Real Egg Product
1 1/4	tablespoons dried parsley
1/2	cup finely chopped scallions
1/2	cup diced celery
1/3	cup diced roasted red bell pepper
2 1/2	teaspoons McCORMICK Old Bay Seasoning
3/4	teaspoon salt
	Pinch black pepper
3	ounces vegetable oil

- ❖ To make sauce, combine roasted pepper puree, shallot, garlic, vinegar and sugar; cover and chill.
- ❖ Toss cornmeal with 1 cup of bread crumbs (1/2 cup bread crumbs for trial recipe); reserve.
- ❖ Combine crabmeat, egg product, parsley, scallions, celery, roasted red pepper, Old Bay Seasoning, salt, pepper and remaining bread crumbs; mix well. Scale mixture into 3-ounce, round, slightly flattened cakes; coat completely with reserved crumb mixture, shaking off excess.
- ❖ Keep crab cakes refrigerated. When needed, sauté each in about 1 tablespoon oil until cooked through.
- ❖ Serve 2 cakes per serving with 2 ounces of sauce. For an appetizer, serve 1 cake with 1 ounce of sauce.

GRILLED SALMON WITH DIJON-MAPLE GINGER BASTING SAUCE

Yield: 12 servings

1 1/2	cups GREY POUPON® Dijon Mustard
1	cup maple syrup
1	teaspoon grated ginger
1	tablespoon minced garlic
1	teaspoon chili oil
	BELLAGIO Olive Oil
12	salmon fillets, skin removed (3 3/4 pounds)

- ❖ To make basting sauce, combine mustard, syrup, ginger, garlic and chili oil; set aside and refrigerate.
- ❖ For each serving, grill a lightly-oiled salmon fillet, flesh side down, for 4 minutes; turn fish and brush with 1 tablespoon sauce. Turn fish again, brush skin side with 1 tablespoon sauce, turn immediately, wait 30 seconds and remove from grill.

SEA LEGS® SEAFOOD AND CRAB SALAD
WITH SESAME LEMON DRESSING

Yield: 12 servings

2	pounds mixed wild greens		*Sesame Lemon Dressing*
1/2	pint red bell pepper, julienned	1	cup cider vinegar
1/2	pint yellow bell pepper, julienned	1	cup vegetable oil
2 1/2	pounds SEA LEGS® Supreme, thawed and flaked	1/4	cup fresh lemon juice
1	cup sliced green onion	1/2	cup honey
	Sesame Lemon Dressing	3	tablespoons minced fresh ginger root
		3	tablespoons sesame oil
		1	tablespoon salt
		2	teaspoons McCORMICK Ground Pepper

- ❖ Combine greens, pepper, Sea Legs® Supreme and green onion in large salad bowl. Toss to mix. Set aside in refrigerator.
- ❖ Arrange individual servings on plate. Drizzle with 2 tablespoons Sesame Lemon Dressing. Serve immediately.

Sesame Lemon Dressing
- ❖ Combine ingredients. Mix well. Makes about 1 pint.

FISH FILLETS PARMESAN

Yield: 4 servings

1/4	cup melted margarine
1	clove garlic, minced
1	pound ARCTIC HARVEST Cod Flounder or other mild whitefish fillets, thawed
1	cup soft bread crumbs
1/3	cup freshly grated Parmesan cheese
	Dill sprigs
	Cherry tomatoes, sliced

- ❖ Preheat broiler. Combine margarine and garlic in flat container; dip fillets in margarine-garlic mixture to coat both sides.
- ❖ Combine bread crumbs and Parmesan cheese on waxed paper; dredge fillets in bread crumbs to thoroughly coat. Place on broiler pan.
- ❖ Broil 6-8 inches from heat for 8-10 minutes until fish flakes easily when tested with a fork. Garnish with dill sprigs and sliced cherry tomatoes.

ICELANDIC SMOKED SALMON
WITH PASTA SHELLS AND GREEN PEAS

Yield: 12 servings

Sauce		1 1/2	pounds SAN GIORGIO Pasta Shells, cooked al dente
2	tablespoons Dijon mustard	24	slices ICELANDIC® Brand Smoked Salmon
2	tablespoons lemon juice	6	ripe tomatoes, seeded and chopped
2	tablespoons dry vermouth	3	cups green peas
1	cup safflower oil or vegetable oil	6	scallions, chopped
1	cup olive oil	3	tablespoons chopped fresh dill
			Freshly ground black pepper

- ❖ In large mixing bowl, whisk mustard, lemon juice and vermouth. Add the oils in a thin stream to form a thick sauce.
- ❖ Add drained, cooked pasta, smoked salmon, tomatoes, peas, scallions, dill and pepper. Toss and chill until ready to serve. Handling instructions for salmon: Keep salmon frozen until ready to serve. Take the fillets out of freezer 4 hours prior to serving. After thawing, do not store product in original packaging. Do not refreeze! In order for the natural oils to generate the full flavor of the salmon, open the package 2 hours before serving.

POULTRY

Lemon Spritz Chicken, page 54

Lemon Spritz Chicken

Skillet Chicken Stew with Corn Dumplings

LEMON SPRITZ CHICKEN

Yield: 12 servings
Serving size: 10 ounces chicken, 2 ounces sauce

5 1/4	pounds TYSON Honey Stung® Fried Chicken (#4432)	4	whole garlic cloves, peeled
		1/2	teaspoon lemon pepper
Lemony White Wine Sauce		1/4	teaspoon cayenne pepper sauce
4 1/2	cups chicken broth	2	tablespoons water
1	cup white wine	2 1/2	tablespoons cornstarch
1/2	cup water	12	fans of lemon slices
1	tablespoon lemon juice, made from concentrate	12	fresh sprigs of thyme
3	tablespoons butter		

- Deep-fry chicken at 350 degrees for 6-8 minutes. Remove from fryer. Drain; keep warm.
- To make wine sauce, combine all ingredients in saucepan. Bring to a boil over high heat. Reduce heat to medium-low and simmer for 30-40 minutes or until liquid is reduced by half. Remove garlic cloves.
- Combine water and cornstarch in small bowl. Add to saucepan. Bring to a boil, stirring constantly. Boil 1 minute. Remove from heat and keep warm.
- To serve, ladle 1/4 cup sauce over chicken. Garnish with a fan of lemon slices and a fresh sprig of thyme.

Serving suggestions: Serve with 1 cup prepared sugar snap peas tossed in herb butter.

SKILLET CHICKEN STEW WITH CORN DUMPLINGS

Yield: 10 servings

36	ounces STOUFFER'S® Creamed Chicken, thawed	1/4	teaspoon McCORMICK Whole Thyme
3	cups milk	1/4	teaspoon McCORMICK Black Pepper
3	teaspoons flour	1	cup all-purpose baking mix
2	cups RYKOFF-SEXTON Frozen Mixed Vegetables	3/4	teaspoon McCORMICK Onion Powder
20	ounces STOUFFER'S® Corn Soufflé, thawed and divided		Pinch pepper
1/3	cup chopped onion		Paprika
1	teaspoon salt, divided		

- In an 18" skillet, combine creamed chicken, milk and flour. Add vegetables, 1 cup of corn soufflé, onion, 3/4 teaspoon salt, thyme and black pepper.
- Cook over medium heat, stirring occasionally, until mixture is simmering.
- While chicken mixture is heating, make dumpling batter. In large bowl, combine baking mix, remaining corn soufflé, 1/4 teaspoon salt, onion powder and pinch black pepper.
- To make dumplings, place a scant 1/4 cup batter into simmering stew for each dumpling (makes 14-15 dumplings).
- Cover skillet and simmer 20-25 minutes on low heat or until dumplings are just firm. Sprinkle dumplings with paprika.

POULTRY

MOROCCAN GRILLED CHICKEN

Yield: 48 servings

1	cup BELLAGIO Olive Oil, divided	5	cups chopped red bell pepper
2	tablespoons McCORMICK Dried Oregano Leaves	5	cups sliced mushrooms
1	tablespoon McCORMICK Ground Allspice	5	cups chopped green onion
1	tablespoon McCORMICK Ground Cumin	1/4	cup minced garlic
1	tablespoon McCORMICK Ground Cloves	1 1/4	teaspoons McCORMICK Cayenne Pepper
48	frozen TYSON Gourmet Skinless Chicken Thigh Fillets (#3175)	1/4	teaspoon coarse-ground McCORMICK Black Pepper
2 1/2	quarts couscous		
3 1/2	quarts low-sodium, defatted chicken broth, boiling		*Red Pimento Sauce*
2/3	cup lemon juice, divided	2	quarts canned pimentos, drained
2/3	cup olive oil, hot	1/2	cup lemon juice

- ❖ Combine 1/4 cup olive oil, oregano, allspice, cumin and cloves in bowl. Mix well.
- ❖ Brush chicken with oregano mixture. Cook on preheated grill over medium heat for 24-29 minutes or until juices run clear when chicken is pierced. Remove from grill. Keep warm.
- ❖ Combine couscous, chicken broth and 2 tablespoons lemon juice in shallow pan. Cover and allow to sit for 10 minutes or until couscous is tender.
- ❖ For pimento sauce, combine hot olive oil, red bell pepper, mushrooms, green onion, garlic, cayenne pepper and black pepper in skillet. Sauté over medium-high heat for 8-10 minutes or until crisp-tender. Remove from heat. Add to couscous and toss well. Keep warm.
- ❖ Combine pimentos and 2 tablespoons lemon juice in food processor bowl. Process for 30-45 seconds or until sauce is smooth. Transfer to covered container. Refrigerate. Serve at room temperature.
- ❖ To serve, portion 3/4 cup couscous mixture on plate. Thinly slice each chicken thigh fillet and fan over couscous. Drizzle 2 tablespoons red pimento sauce over chicken.

Serving suggestion: Serve with crusty bread.

CHICKEN CACCIATORE

Yield: 50 servings

25	pounds chicken parts	1	tablespoon garlic powder
4	pounds fresh mushrooms	3	(50 ounce) cans CAMPBELL'S® Condensed Tomato Soup
1	pound sliced onion	3	cups water
1/4	cup crushed basil leaves	1	teaspoon pepper
1/4	cup crushed oregano leaves	6	pounds, 2 ounces spaghetti

- ❖ In large saucepot, cook chicken until browned. In each of 4 baking pans (12"x 20" x 2"), evenly divide chicken.
- ❖ Add mushrooms, onion, basil, oregano and garlic powder to saucepot and cook until tender.
- ❖ Add soup, water and pepper. Heat to a boil. Pour 1 1/2 quarts plus 1/2 cup soup mixture over each pan. Cover.
- ❖ Bake at 400 degrees for 45 minutes or until chicken is no longer pink. Stir sauce.
- ❖ Cook spaghetti without added salt; rinse and drain.
- ❖ Portion chicken over 1 cup hot spaghetti. Using 4-ounce ladle, portion sauce over all.

Chicken Rojas

Honey-Spiced Glazed Turkey

CHICKEN ROJAS

Yield: 50 servings

50	boneless, skinless chicken breasts
6	quarts *Southwestern Black Refried Beans*
3	pounds *Tortilla Straw*
100	slices tomato
6	cups OLD EL PASO Green Chili Strip, heated
6	quarts *Rojas Sauce*
3	pounds Monterey Jack Cheese, grated
25	ounces green onion, sliced

<u>Southwestern Black Refried Beans</u>

1	#10 can OLD EL PASO Black Refried Beans
1	quart OLD EL PASO Picante Sauce
2	cups finely chopped onion
2	cups diced tomato
2	cups OLD EL PASO Chopped Green Chilies

<u>Tortilla Straw</u>

48	(6") OLD EL PASO Corn Tortillas

<u>Rojas Sauce</u>

3	quarts OLD EL PASO Enchilada Sauce
3	quarts OLD EL PASO Picante Sauce

- ❖ Grill chicken breasts until done.
- ❖ Spread beans on a dinner plate, top with Tortilla Straw and place chicken breasts on top.
- ❖ Arrange tomato slices and green chili strips on top of chicken, ladle Rojas Sauce over chicken breasts and sprinkle with cheese. Place under cheese melter to melt cheese. Sprinkle with green onion.

<u>Southwestern Black Refried Beans</u>
- ❖ Blend all ingredients together in a saucepan, bring to a boil, remove from heat and hold warm for service.

<u>Tortilla Straw</u>
- ❖ Cut tortillas crosswise, $1/4$" wide into long, thin strips.
- ❖ Place in deep fat fryer at 350 degrees and fry for approximately 1 minute or until they begin to brown.
- ❖ Place in a bowl lined with a towel and cover until needed.

Note: Tortilla Straw can be made before service time and held at room temperature.

<u>Rojas Sauce</u>
- ❖ Combine ingredients together and bring to a boil. Hold for service.

POULTRY

HONEY-SPICED GLAZED TURKEY

Yield: 50 servings
Serving size: 3 ounces sliced turkey and ½ cup rice

12	pounds JENNIE-O® Oven Roasted Half Turkey Breast or Grand Champion Hickory Smoked Turkey Breast	4	pounds wild rice or long grain and wild rice blend
2	cups honey	1	gallon water
3	tablespoons minced garlic, divided	½	cup poultry stock base
2	tablespoons TULKOFF'S Prepared Horseradish	½	pound chopped pecans
4	teaspoons McCORMICK Ground Ginger	½	pound golden raisins
4	teaspoons McCORMICK Marjoram Leaves	3	pounds cranberry relish (optional)

❖ For oven roasted half breasts: carve thawed breasts into 1-ounce slices.
   For hickory smoked breasts: slice thawed breasts in half lengthwise and carve each half into 1-ounce slices.
❖ Shingle sliced turkey into shallow counter pans.
❖ Combine honey, half the garlic, horseradish, ginger and marjoram. Drizzle evenly over turkey breast slices.
❖ Cover and place into a 350-degree oven; heat to service temperature.
❖ Meanwhile, combine rice, water, base and remaining garlic. Bring to a boil, then simmer, covered, for 45 minutes or until rice is tender; drain off any remaining liquid. Add pecans and raisins; toss.
❖ Serve 3 ounces sliced turkey with ½ cup rice mixture. Garnish with cranberry relish, if desired.

FAJITA CHICKEN PASTA SALAD

Yield: 48 servings

2	gallons TYSON Flavor-Redi® Breast Fajita Strips, thawed (#6119)*	2½	quarts coarsely chopped red bell pepper
1½	gallons SAN GIORGIO Rotini Pasta, cooked	1	quart chopped green onion
2½	quarts coarsely chopped zucchini	1	quart RYKOFF-SEXTON Low-Calorie Italian Dressing
2½	quarts coarsely chopped yellow squash	2	cups light mayonnaise
		20	heads romaine lettuce, leaves separated
			Minced parsley

❖ Combine chicken, pasta, zucchini, squash, pepper and onion in large bowl.
❖ Combine Italian dressing and mayonnaise in bowl. Stir well. Pour over chicken mixture. Toss to coat, cover and refrigerate.
❖ To serve, portion lettuce leaves on each plate and top with 1½ cups chicken fajita mixture. Garnish with parsley.

Serving suggestion: Serve with crispy breadsticks.

*Can substitute #6111 TYSON Fully Cooked Quik-to-Fix® Beef Fajita Strips, #6127 TYSON Fully Cooked Quik-to-Fix Naturally Shaped Beef Fajita Strips or #3002 TYSON Diced White Fryer Meat (¾" diced) for patrons who prefer less spicy food.

Variations: This popular pasta salad is prepared quickly with fully cooked breast fajita strips and a fresh or frozen vegetable mix. The signature dressing adds the right amount of mayonnaise and Italian dressing to bind ingredients and spark flavor.
Instead of pasta, try stuffing a fresh tomato with crunchy fajita chicken salad mixture. Another innovative twist is to fill cooled pasta shells with the cold and colorful mixture and serve on a bed of crisp romaine lettuce. (The pasta shells also work as appetizers.)
Any type of dressing or prepared sauce can be substituted for dressing, including bleu cheese, ranch, thousand island and honey mustard. For an Oriental twist, use prepared sweet and sour or peanut sauce. To extend fajita flavor, mix mayonnaise with mild salsa.
Cold salads hold well for take-out and deli. Package salad in single-serving containers with crispy breadsticks or crackers.

BARBECUE CHICKEN QUESADILLAS

Yield: 10 servings
Serving size: 1 quesadilla

1½	pounds RYKOFF-SEXTON Diced Cooked Chicken Breast	½	teaspoon McCORMICK Granulated Garlic
1	cup barbecue sauce	10	(9") flour tortillas
6	ounces Wisconsin Cheddar cheese, grated	1	cup canned black beans, rinsed
6	ounces Monterey Jack cheese, grated	½	cup diced red bell pepper
1	cup sliced scallions, divided	2	cups guacamole
1	tablespoon chili powder	1	cup dairy sour cream
¾	teaspoon McCORMICK Ground Cumin	20	cilantro sprigs

❖ Combine chicken, barbecue sauce, Cheddar and Monterey Jack cheeses, ¾ cup scallions and seasonings.
❖ Spread chicken mixture over half of each tortilla, spreading to edge. Fold plain half over filling, press down firmly.
❖ Cook tortillas in dry skillet until crisp and lightly browned, turning once.
❖ For each portion, cut quesadilla into 6 wedges. Place on serving plate, points toward center. Place combined beans, red bell pepper and cup scallions in center. Top with guacamole, sour cream and cilantro.

Thai Chicken

Honey-Ginger Glazed Cornish Hen

THAI CHICKEN

Yield: 12 servings
Serving size: 16 ounces

2	cups FLEISCHMANN'S® Egg Beaters® Real Egg Product, divided	4	teaspoons McCORMICK Grated Ginger
		1/2	teaspoon McCORMICK Red Pepper Flakes
2 1/4	pounds boneless, skinless chicken, 1-ounce pieces (1/2" thick)	1/4	teaspoon McCORMICK Black Pepper
		1 1/2	quarts chicken stock
	Salt	1	cup coconut cream
	Pepper	5	tablespoons lime juice
2 1/2	cups cornstarch	1/3	cup canned, diced tomato
2/3	cup peanut oil	1/4	cup chopped fresh cilantro
4	cups sliced onion	12	cups cooked brown rice
1	tablespoon McCORMICK Minced Garlic		

❖ Using a 2-ounce ladle, pour 8, 1/4-cup portions of egg product onto a lightly greased, medium-high heat griddle. Cook until browned on both sides. Remove, roll and cut into thin strips; reserve.

❖ Season chicken with salt and pepper, dust with cornstarch and shake off excess. Dip in remaining egg product to coat evenly and allow excess to drain off. Dust again with cornstarch.

❖ Sauté immediately in hot peanut oil, place on paper towel and keep warm. In the same pan, remove all but 1 tablespoon of oil. Sauté onion, garlic, ginger, red pepper flakes and black pepper until onion is translucent. Add stock and coconut cream; reduce by half. Add lime juice, tomato, cilantro and reserved chicken; simmer until chicken is heated.

❖ Serve 3 ounces of chicken and 3 ounces of sauce over 1 cup of brown rice; garnish with reserved strips of egg product.

HONEY-GINGER GLAZED CORNISH HEN

Yield: 12 servings
Serving size: 7 ounces Cornish hen, 3 ounces pasta

12	frozen TYSON Cornish Hen Halves (#6907)	1/4	cup soy sauce
		1	tablespoon minced ginger root
Sherry-Soy-Honey Glaze		1	tablespoon minced garlic
1	cup dry sherry	2	teaspoons salt
1	cup minced onion		
1/3	cup honey	2 1/4	pounds vermicelli or spaghetti, cooked al dente

❖ Place hens in baking pan, breast side up.

❖ To make glaze, combine ingredients in bowl and mix well. Pour over hens. Bake in preheated conventional oven at 375 degrees for 1 1/2-2 hours or until juices run clear when hens are pierced. Baste occasionally with pan juices during cooking.

❖ Remove from oven. Transfer hens to clean pan and keep warm. Strain pan juices into saucepan and discard solids. Cook over high heat for 7-10 minutes or until reduced by half, stirring constantly. Pour sauce evenly over hens; keep warm.

❖ To prepare to order, reheat pasta in boiling water for 10-20 seconds. Drain. Serve each hen on a bed of 3 ounces of pasta.

BARBECUE CHICKEN WITH DIJON MASHED POTATOES

Yield: 20 halves

20	TYSON Chicken Halves		*Dijon Mashed Potatoes*
	Oil	8	pounds potatoes, peeled
5	cups CATTLEMEN'S Classic Sauce	1 3/4	cups milk
	Dijon Mashed Potatoes	1	cup butter
		2	teaspoons salt
		1	cup FRENCH'S Dijon Mustard
		1/4	cup chopped fresh parsley

- Brush chicken lightly with oil before placing on grill, rotisserie or in medium oven. Smoked chicken should be done in a 300-350 degree section of smoker.
- Depending on cooking method and bird weight, cooking takes about 40 minutes-1 1/2 hours. When done, thermometer inserted into thigh should register 165 degrees or juices should run clear when pierced with fork or knife just under thigh.
- Brush on sauce only during last 15 minutes, to prevent caramelization and burning.
- Serve with Dijon Mashed Potatoes.

Dijon Mashed Potatoes

- Boil potatoes until fork tender, about 30 minutes. Drain liquid from potatoes.
- Add milk, butter and salt. Whip. Fold in Dijon mustard and parsley.
- Serve or transfer to serving pan and cover until service.

TURKEY TERIYAKI WITH SESAME NOODLES

Yield: 24 servings
Serving size: 4 ounces teriyaki, 1 cup noodles

1 1/2	cups soy sauce	1	teaspoon red pepper flakes
1/2	cup rice wine vinegar	1	cup dark sesame oil
1/3	cup minced fresh ginger root	1	cup vegetable oil
1/3	cup minced fresh cilantro	6	quarts cooked linguini, drained
1/4	cup honey	1/2	cup toasted sesame seeds
2	tablespoons minced garlic	6	pounds WAMPLER-LONGACRE Turkey Teriyaki, hot

- In bowl, combine soy sauce, vinegar, ginger, cilantro, honey, garlic and red pepper flakes; mix well. Stir in oils; cover and let stand at least 2 hours before using as a sauce to toss with pasta. To serve, toss pasta with sauce. Serve approximately 1 cup pasta per serving; top with 1 teaspoon sesame seeds and 4 ounces hot turkey teriyaki.

Serving suggestion: Serve with steamed snow peas and julienned red bell pepper.

TURKEY SAUSAGE KABOBS

Yield: 24 appetizer servings
Serving size: 2 ounces turkey, 1 appetizer kabob

3/4	cup white wine vinegar	1	medium red bell pepper, cut into chunks
2	tablespoons minced garlic	1	medium green bell pepper, cut into chunks
	Thyme	24	medium mushrooms, halved
3/4	cup olive oil	3	bunches green onion, trimmed
24	WAMPLER-LONGACRE Turkey Italian Sausage		

- In bowl, combine vinegar, garlic, thyme and oil; mix well, cover and let stand 1 hour before using as a marinade and basting sauce.
- Cut turkey sausages into 3 chunks each. Weave onto 8" bamboo skewers, along with pepper chunks, mushrooms and green onion. On each skewer, place 3 sausage chunks, 3-4 pepper chunks, 2 mushroom halves and a 1" x 5" piece of green onion. Brush each kabob with 1 teaspoon marinade.
- Grill each kabob to order, 2-3 minutes per side or until cooked through.

POULTRY

Turkey Breast with Yam Bake

Turkey Scaloppini with Warm Cranberry Vinaigrette

TURKEY BREAST WITH YAM BAKE

Yield: 72 servings
Serving size: 2 ounces sliced turkey, 4 ounces yam bake

2	#10 cans CARBOTROL Juicee Yams
1	#10 can CARBOTROL Mandarin Oranges
1	#10 can CARBOTROL Pineapple Tidbits
1/4	cup grated orange rind
1/2	cup margarine
1	cup brown sugar
1	cup juice (reserved from pineapple tidbits)
1/2	teaspoon salt
2	teaspoons McCORMICK Cinnamon
9	pounds PINE RIDGE FARMS Sliced Cooked Turkey

- Drain juice from yams and pour yams into 12" x 20" x 2" pan.
- Drain juice from mandarin oranges and pineapple tidbits, reserving one cup from pineapple tidbits.
- Pour drained mandarin oranges and pineapple tidbits over yams and sprinkle with grated orange rind.
- Combine margarine, brown sugar, reserved juice from pineapple tidbits, salt and cinnamon in saucepan. Heat to boiling and simmer 5 minutes.
- Pour sauce over yams, mandarin oranges and pineapple tidbits.
- Bake at 350 degrees for 30 minutes.
- Serve with hot, sliced turkey.

TURKEY SCALOPPINI WITH WARM CRANBERRY VINAIGRETTE

Yield: 4 servings

2	(4 ounce) WAMPLER-LONGACRE Turkey Breast Chops or TenderSteak™, butterflied
1/4	cup seasoned flour
1	ounce BELLAGIO Extra Virgin Olive Oil
1	ounce red wine vinegar
1/3	cup dried cranberries
1	ounce veal glace
1	tablespoon honey
1/2	cup heavy cream
3/4	cup wild greens
1	cup warm cranberry vinaigrette

- Slice turkey thinly, dredge in seasoned flour and sauté in olive oil until brown and cooked through. Remove and keep warm.
- In same pan, de-glaze with vinegar and add cranberries, veal glace and honey. Simmer 2 minutes. Add cream and reduce by 1/2.
- Place turkey on plates and top with warm vinaigrette.

POULTRY

SIDE DISHES & BREADS

Spinach Torte, page 62

Spinach Torte

Heartland Chicken Casserole

SPINACH TORTE

Yield: 12 servings
Serving size: 6 ounces

1/4	pound onion, chopped	1/2	pound onion, chopped
2	tablespoons minced garlic	4	tablespoons minced garlic
2	tablespoons olive oil	4	tablespoons olive oil
1	pound part-skim ricotta cheese	2	pounds part-skim ricotta cheese
1 1/2	quarts FLEISCHMANN'S® Egg Beaters® Real Egg Product, divided	3	quarts FLEISCHMANN'S® Egg Beaters® Real Egg Product, divided
3/4	pound frozen spinach, thawed, chopped and squeezed dry	1 1/2	pounds frozen spinach, thawed, chopped and squeezed dry
3	ounces raisins, packed and coarsely chopped	6	ounces raisins, packed and coarsely chopped
1/2	pound bread crumbs	1	pound bread crumbs
3	ounces Parmesan cheese, grated and divided	6	ounces Parmesan cheese, grated and divided
1	teaspoon ground sage	2	teaspoons ground sage
1/2	teaspoon McCORMICK Ground Nutmeg	1	teaspoon ground nutmeg
1/2	teaspoon dried marjoram leaf	1	teaspoon dried marjoram leaf
1	teaspoon McCORMICK Black Pepper	2	teaspoons McCORMICK Black Pepper
2	teaspoons salt	4	teaspoons salt

Yield: 24 servings
Serving size: 6 ounces

❖ Sauté onion and garlic in olive oil until golden. Set aside.

❖ In a blender or food processor, puree ricotta cheese with 2 cups egg product (1 cup for trial recipe) until smooth. Pour into a mixing bowl and add spinach, raisins, bread crumbs, 1/2 cup Parmesan cheese (1/4 cup for trial recipe), sage, nutmeg, marjoram, pepper, salt, reserved onion, garlic and remaining egg product; beat until thoroughly combined.

❖ Pour into 2 lightly greased, half hotel pans (1 half hotel pan for trial recipe); sprinkle with remaining Parmesan cheese and bake at 325 degrees for 1 hour until a knife inserted in center comes out clean. Allow to cool for 10 minutes, and cut into 24 portions (12 portions for trial recipe).

HEARTLAND CHICKEN CASSEROLE

Yield: 12 servings
Serving size: 7 ounces

6	tablespoons melted butter	2	cups commercially prepared white sauce
2	cups diced onion	2	cups elbow macaroni, cooked
1	cup diced carrots	1	cup diced tomato, drained
1	cup diced celery	1	cup cubed Cheddar cheese (3/4")
2	teaspoons salt	1/2	cup chicken stock
1 1/2	teaspoons minced garlic	2	teaspoons poultry seasoning
1 1/2	pounds frozen TYSON Pulled Natural Proportion Fryer Meat (#2037)		

❖ Combine butter, onion, carrots, celery, salt and garlic in skillet. Sauté over medium-low heat for 12-15 minutes or until vegetables are tender, but not browned. Remove from heat. Transfer to a bowl.

❖ Add remaining ingredients to vegetable mixture. Stir well. Transfer to greased baking pan.

SIDE DISHES & BREADS

CHICKEN AND RICE AU VIN

Yield: 40 servings
Serving size: 6 ounces

2	(49½ ounce) cans SWEET SUE Chicken Broth	4	cups white wine
4¾	cups rice	1	pound mushrooms, sliced
1	tablespoon garlic salt	1	cup chopped red bell pepper
1	(50 ounce) can SWEET SUE Deluxe Boned Chicken	1	cup chopped onion
½	cup butter	¼	cup butter
½	cup flour	3	cups bread crumbs
2¼	cups milk		

- Reserve 2 cups chicken broth; set aside.
- Cook rice in remaining broth and garlic salt. Place cooked rice in a greased full steam table pan.
- Spread chicken over rice.
- Make white sauce: melt butter and stir in flour. Continue stirring and cook for one minute. Gradually stir in 2 cups reserved broth, milk and white wine. Cook, stirring until thickened.
- Stir in mushrooms, red bell pepper and onion. Pour evenly over chicken.
- Melt butter and toss with bread crumbs. Sprinkle over sauce.
- Bake at 350 degrees for 45 minutes.

Note: A dry white sauce mix may be used, with broth and white wine as liquids.

GRECIAN RICE

Yield: 30 servings

1	box NEAR EAST Rice Pilaf (2 pounds, 4 ounces), uncooked	1½	cups RYKOFF-SEXTON Italian Dressing
¼	cup BELLAGIO Olive Oil	1	cup chopped fresh parsley
1	pound onion, thinly sliced	⅓	cup RYKOFF-SEXTON Lemon Juice
2	pounds gyro meat, cooked and diced (optional)		Romaine lettuce
2¼	cups drained and chopped pimentos		Cucumber sauce

- Prepare rice according to package directions.
- Melt olive oil in large skillet. Sauté onions until transparent.
- Combine cooked rice with sautéed onions, meat, pimento, dressing, parsley and lemon juice. Toss lightly until well-combined.
- The final cooking temperature is at or above 165 degrees. Serve hot or well-chilled.
- Garnish with romaine lettuce and cucumber sauce.

Variation: Substitute cooked chicken for cooked gyro meat.

Time-saving tips: Prepare rice 24 hours in advance. Cool rice to 45 degrees or below within 4 hours in shallow pans with a product depth of less than 2 inches under refrigeration. Stir frequently.

Holding time: Hold at 140 degrees or above in steam table at medium heat (#5) for 3 hours. Reheat rice one time only to 165 degrees or above within 2 hours.

SHRIMP AND WILD RICE CASSEROLE

Yield: 6 servings

1½	cups sliced mushrooms	1	(10¾ ounce) can low-sodium condensed cream of shrimp soup
2	ribs celery, sliced		
1	small onion, chopped	2	teaspoons Worcestershire sauce
1	tablespoon olive oil	2	ounces chopped pimentos, drained and divided
12	ounces ASIAN HARVEST Medium Shrimp		Parsley sprigs
2	cups cooked wild rice (½ cup uncooked)		

- Heat oven to 375 degrees.
- Sauté mushrooms, celery and onion in olive oil until tender and lightly browned. Combine with remaining ingredients using half of pimentos. Pour mixture into 8" x 8" casserole.
- Bake for 30-35 minutes until bubbly. Garnish with remaining pimentos and parsley sprigs.

Side Dishes & Breads

ISO A LA PESTO RICE

Yield: 22 servings
Serving size: 1 cup

1	box NEAR EAST Chicken Flavor Rice Pilaf, uncooked	1	cup grated Parmesan cheese
2	cups pesto sauce		Fresh basil leaves
4	ounces sun-dried tomatoes, marinated in oil, drained and shredded		Pine nuts

- ❖ *Prepare rice according to package directions, except omit margarine or butter.*
- ❖ *Transfer to large mixing bowl. Stir in pesto, tomatoes and cheese.*
- ❖ *The final cooking temperature is at or above 165 degrees. Serve hot or well-chilled.*
- ❖ *Garnish with fresh basil leaves and pine nuts.*

Variation: Substitute Romano cheese for Parmesan cheese.

Time-saving tips: Prepare rice 24 hours in advance. Cool rice to 45 degrees or below within 4 hours in shallow pans with a product depth of less than 2 inches under refrigeration. Stir frequently.

Holding time: Hold at 140 degrees or above in steam table at medium heat (#5) for up to 3 hours. Reheat rice one time only to 165 degrees or above within 2 hours.

CALICO CHUCKWAGON RICE

Yield: 25 servings

1	box NEAR EAST Spanish Rice (2 pounds, 4 ounces), uncooked	2	pounds frozen corn, red pepper, green pepper and onion blend
2	pounds ground beef, cooked and drained (optional)	$2^{3/4}$	cups barbecue sauce
			Cheddar cheese, grated

- ❖ *Prepare rice according to package directions; except omit margarine or butter.*
- ❖ *Brown beef and cover; set aside.*
- ❖ *Cook vegetables according to package directions.*
- ❖ *In large bowl, combine hot cooked rice, cooked beef, vegetables and barbecue sauce. Toss lightly until ingredients are well-combined.*
- ❖ *The final cooking temperature is at or above 165 degrees. Serve hot.*
- ❖ *Garnish with grated Cheddar cheese.*

Variation: Substitute ground turkey for ground beef.

Time-saving tips: Prepare rice 24 hours in advance. Cool rice to 45 degrees or below within 4 hours in shallow pans with a product depth of less than 2 inches under refrigeration. Stir frequently.

Holding time: Hold at 140 degrees or above in steam table at medium heat (#5) for up to 3 hours. Reheat rice one time only to 165 degrees or above within 2 hours.

COZUMEL FAJITA RICE

Yield: 34 servings
Serving size: 1 cup

1	box NEAR EAST Spanish Rice (2 pounds, 4 ounces), uncooked	$1/4$	cup BELLAGIO Olive Oil
$3^{1/2}$	cups diced red bell pepper	2	pounds flanked beef, cooked and cut in strips (optional)
$3^{1/2}$	cups diced green bell pepper	3	cups drained chunky PACE Salsa
1	pound, 8 ounces onion, thinly sliced		Cilantro sprigs

- ❖ *Prepare rice according to package directions; except omit margarine and butter.*
- ❖ *Lightly sauté bell pepper and onion in olive oil until onion is transparent.*
- ❖ *Toss cooked rice, sautéed vegetables, meat and salsa. The final cooking temperature is at or above 165 degrees. Serve hot.*
- ❖ *Garnish with cilantro sprigs.*

Variation: May substitute chicken strips for beef strips.

Time-saving tips: Prepare rice 24 hours in advance. Cool rice to 45 degrees or below within 4 hours in shallow pans with a product depth of less than 2 inches under refrigeration. Stir frequently.

Holding time: Hold at 140 degrees or above in steam table at medium heat (#5) for up to 3 hours. Reheat rice one time only to 165 degrees or above within 2 hours.

SIDE DISHES & BREADS

ROSARITA'S CHEESE 'N' CHILI ENCHILADAS

Yield: 6 servings

	WESSON® CRYSTAL® Shortening
6	(6") corn tortillas
1 1/2	cups grated Cheddar cheese
1 1/2	cups grated Monterey Jack cheese
1/2	cup ROSARITA® Diced Green Chilies
1/2	cup drained, sliced ripe olives
2 1/2	cups ROSARITA® Enchilada Sauce

- ❖ In deep fat fryer or skillet, heat oil to 350 degrees. Fry each tortilla for a few seconds to soften; drain well.
- ❖ In bowl, combine cheeses, green chilies and olives; set aside.
- ❖ For small batch: in 8" x 8" x 2" pan, pour 4 ounces enchilada sauce.
- ❖ For large batch: in each of 2 (2" deep) full-size hotel pans, pour 8 ounces enchilada sauce.
- ❖ In bowl, pour remaining enchilada sauce and dip each tortilla in sauce to coat.
- ❖ Place 1 1/2 ounces cheese mixture on each tortilla, roll to enclose filling; place enchiladas seam side down in pan(s).
- ❖ Pour remaining sauce over enchiladas in pan(s), dividing evenly between full-size hotel pans for large batch.
- ❖ Sprinkle each pan with remaining cheese mixture, dividing evenly between full-size pans for large batch.
- ❖ Bake in preheated oven at 350 degrees—30 minutes for small batch or 45 minutes for large batch or until cheese is melted.

BLACK BEAN AND CHEESE ENCHILADAS

Yield: 50 servings

100	OLD EL PASO 6" Corn Tortillas
6 1/4	quarts Mexican Black Bean Dip
50	ounces onion, diced
9 1/3	pounds Monterey Jack cheese, grated
6 1/4	quarts OLD EL PASO Enchilada Sauce, heated
12 1/2	cups OLD EL PASO Thick 'N Chunky Salsa (medium or mild)

Mexican Black Bean Dip — Yield: 6 quarts

1	#10 can OLD EL PASO Black Refried Beans
3	cups OLD EL PASO Picante Sauce (medium or mild)
2	cups finely chopped onions
1	(27 ounce) can OLD EL PASO Green Chilies, chopped

- ❖ Dip tortillas into hot fryer long enough to make tortillas soft and pliable. After dipping, allow to drain completely.
- ❖ Place tortillas on counter and place 2 ounces of bean mixture in a line across center of tortilla, sprinkle with 1/2 ounce of onion and top with 1 ounce of grated cheese. Roll up.
- ❖ Portion 2 enchiladas on a plate, cover and refrigerate until needed.
- ❖ To order, place in the microwave for approximately 1 minute, uncover and ladle 3 ounces of hot enchilada sauce over the top. Sprinkle with remaining cheese and melt. Garnish with salsa.

Mexican Black Bean Dip
- ❖ Blend all ingredients together thoroughly; cover and refrigerate until needed.

Rosarita's Cheese 'n' Chili Enchiladas

Black Bean and Cheese Enchiladas

Side Dishes & Breads

CREAMY VEGETABLE MEDLEY

Yield: 50 servings
Serving size: 1/2 cup

3	pounds, 8 ounces frozen broccoli cuts
3	pounds, 8 ounces frozen sliced carrots
3	pounds, 8 ounces frozen cauliflower flowerets
2	(50 ounce) cans CAMPBELL'S® Condensed Cream of Celery Soup
2	teaspoons onion powder
2	teaspoons crushed thyme leaves
1/2	teaspoon pepper

- Cook vegetables. Drain; set aside.
- In large sauce pot, mix soup, onion powder, thyme and pepper. Heat to a boil, stirring occasionally.
- Add vegetables. Heat through.
- Portion using No. 8 scoop (1/2 cup).

CURRIED DIJON GRILLED VEGETABLE RISOTTO

Yield: 32 servings
Serving size: 8 ounces

10	ounces eggplant, sliced 1/2"
1 1/2	pounds red and yellow bell pepper, halved
1/2	pound onion, sliced 1/2"
3/4	pound zucchini, sliced 1/2"
1/2	teaspoon ground black pepper, divided
3/4	teaspoon ground cumin, divided
3/4	teaspoon ground coriander, divided
3/4	teaspoon ground curry powder, divided
	Vegetable oil spray
11	ounces bulgur wheat
1/2	cup chopped almonds
11	ounces brown rice
1/2	cup COLLEGE INN® Lower Sodium Chicken Broth
3 1/4	quarts coarsely chopped chickpeas
5	ounces golden raisins
1 1/4	cups GREY POUPON® Dijon Mustard
	Parsley, chopped

- In large bowl, toss eggplant, peppers, onion and zucchini with 1/4 teaspoon of pepper, cumin, coriander and curry powder; coat lightly with oil spray and grill for 4-5 minutes. Remove from grill and dice into 1/2" pieces; set aside.
- In medium sauté pan, toast bulgur wheat and almonds; set aside.
- In large stockpot over medium-high heat, combine the brown rice, chicken broth, reserved vegetables and remaining cumin, coriander and curry powder; bring to a boil, then simmer covered for 45 minutes. Add chickpeas, raisins, Dijon mustard, reserved toasted bulgur wheat and almonds; simmer covered for an additional 5 minutes. Hold on a steam table until needed for service, adding stock if necessary.
- Garnish with parsley and serve.

FESTIVE HAM DRESSING

Yield: 25 thick servings, 50 thin servings*

12	cups jalapeño cornbread
2	cups diced onion
2	cups diced celery
1/2	cup butter
8	slices bread, cubed
2	cups raisins
3 1/2	cups crushed pineapple, with juice
1	#10 can BRYAN Ham Shanks, with juice (6 pounds, 6 ounces)
2	cups pineapple juice
4	eggs, beaten
2	teaspoons pepper

- Crumble jalapeño cornbread into large bowl. Sauté onion and celery in butter until onion is clear. Add onion mixture and all remaining ingredients to cornbread. Mix well.
- Pour into greased 12" x 20" x 2" steam table pan. Bake at 400 degrees until set.

*Makes a thick dressing (2"-2 1/2" thick). For thinner portions, divide between two steam table pans (1" thick). Cut cooking time to 20 minutes.

SIDE DISHES & BREADS

AMERICAN RYE BREAD

80%	Iron Duke®
20%	000 rye flour
2%	salt
2%	shortening
1%	diastatic malt syrup
2%	yeast (compressed)
58%	water (variable)

- Mix all ingredients for 3-4 minutes on medium speed.
- Dough temperature is 76 degrees.
- Fermentation time: 2 hours to bench. Scaling weight: 10 ounces/loaf, round up. Proof 30 minutes.
- Form into loaves. Proof approximately 50 minutes.
- Bake at 425 degrees. Use steam during baking.

MILWAUKEE DARK RYE BREAD

80%	IRON DUKE®
20%	HOFFMULLER Rye Flour
2%	salt
2%	shortening
1%	diastatic malt syrup
2%	yeast (compressed)
58%	water (variable)
2%	dark molasses
	Caramel coloring (optional)

- Mix all ingredients for 3-4 minutes on medium speed.
- Dough temperature is 76 degrees.
- Fermentation time: 2 hours to bench. Scaling weight: 10 ounces/loaf, round up. Proof 30 minutes.
- Form into loaves. Proof approximately 50 minutes.
- Bake at 425 degrees. Use steam during baking.
- Sponge system: Mix a portion of flour (roughly 60%) and water (roughly 55%) with all yeast. Ferment dough 3-5 hours. Return to mixer, add balance of ingredients and mix to a developed dough. Rest 20-30 minutes. Divide and scale in usual manner.

VIENNA BREAD

100%	ALL TRUMPS® Remarkable® GM Superlative®
2%	salt
3%	sugar
3%	nonfat dry milk
2.5%	yeast (compressed)
3%	shortening
60%	water

- Mix all ingredients for 4-6 minutes on medium speed.
- Fermentation time: 2 hours to bench, scale 18 ounces, round up and proof 30 minutes.
- Form into loaves. Place on boards/pans dusted with cornmeal.
- Proof approximately 50-60 minutes. Give proofed loaves several slashes (4-5) across loaf with a sharp knife.
- Bake at 425 degrees. Use full steam at beginning of bake. Reduce steam when loaves are fully expanded and begin to color. Bake time is approximately 25 minutes.

Side Dishes & Breads

Parmesan Garlic Cheese Bread

Kaiser Rolls/Bread Sticks

PARMESAN GARLIC CHEESE BREAD

Yield: 48 slices

32	ounces PHASE® Liquid Butter Alternative
3½	ounces garlic powder
6	loaves French bread
2	pounds Parmesan cheese, grated
2	cups chopped fresh parsley
2	ounces paprika

- ❖ Combine Phase® and garlic.
- ❖ Cut bread into 1" slices, brush with Phase®/garlic mixture and arrange on sheet pan.
- ❖ Sprinkle bread with Parmesan cheese, parsley and paprika. Place sheet pan under broiler until brown (approximately 2-3 minutes).

KAISER ROLLS/BREAD STICKS

100%	ALL TRUMPS®
2%	salt
4%	sugar
2%	diastatic malt syrup
5%	liquid whole egg
4%	vegetable oil
3%	yeast (compressed)
60%	water

- ❖ Mix time: 4-6 minutes, medium speed.
- ❖ Dough temperature: 76-78 degrees.
- ❖ Fermentation time: 2½ hours punch, 30 minutes bench.
- ❖ Scaled dough pieces should weigh 3 ounces for kaiser roll, ½ ounce for bread sticks.
- ❖ Place rounded units on bench. Keep covered to prevent crusting. Rest 30 minutes.
- ❖ Make into kaiser rolls either by hand or by using a kaiser roll cutter.
- ❖ For bread sticks, roll out to approximately ¼" - ⅜" diameter (to resemble a pencil).
- ❖ Proof approximately 1 hour. Bake at 425 degrees. Use steam during baking.

SIDE DISHES & BREADS

PIZZA & PASTA

Spinach Lasagna Magnifico, page 75

AMAZIN' A.M. PIZZA

Yield: 12 servings

3/4	pound ham, diced (1/4")	12	(6") prepared pizza shells
3/4	pound tomato, diced (1/4")	2 1/4	quarts FLEISCHMANN'S® Egg Beaters® Real Egg Product, room temperature
3/4	pound reduced-fat Cheddar cheese, grated		

❖ Combine ham, tomato and Cheddar cheese; mix well. Top each pizza shell with 3 ounces of mixture, cover and refrigerate until needed for service.

❖ For each serving, ladle 6 ounces egg product onto a lightly greased, medium heat griddle. Slowly stir egg product until they are set but still soft and moist.

❖ Meanwhile, place a reserved ham and cheese pizza in a 400-degree oven for 5-10 minutes, until cheese melts. Top with egg product and serve immediately.

WISCONSIN WHITE CHEDDAR PIZZA WITH BACON, WALNUTS AND SAGE

Yield: 2 (9") pizzas, 4 servings

Crust
1	cup water
2	cups all-purpose flour
1/2	cup cornmeal
1	tablespoon minced fresh sage leaves
1	package (2 1/4 teaspoons) instant dry yeast
1	teaspoon salt
1	teaspoon sugar
2	tablespoons BELLAGIO Olive Oil

Pizza
8	ounces HORMEL Sliced Smoked Bacon, chopped
8	ounces Wisconsin White Cheddar Cheese, grated
4	ounces walnuts, toasted and chopped
	Italian parsley leaves, loosely packed

❖ Heat water to 120-130 degrees.

❖ Mix 1 cup of flour, cornmeal, sage, yeast, salt and sugar. Add water and oil. Mix until almost smooth. Gradually add enough remaining flour to make a firm dough. Knead 5 minutes. Cover with a damp cloth and allow to rise in warm place until double in size, about 1 hour. Punch dough down; allow to rise one more time.

❖ Cook bacon until done, but not crisp. Drain on paper towels.

❖ Divide dough in half, roll or press each into 9" circle. Place on baking sheet. Top each with Wisconsin White Cheddar cheese, bacon and walnuts.

❖ Bake at 500 degrees 8-10 minutes or until dough is done. Sprinkle with parsley.

Variations: Upscale—Use blend of four Wisconsin cheeses: Cheddar, Gorgonzola, Asiago and Fontina. Substitute cooked, chopped duck for bacon.

Vegetarian—Eliminate bacon. Add sliced apples or pears. For cheeses, use a blend of grated Wisconsin Havarti and grated Cheddar.

Appetizer—Place toppings on small-size prepared focaccia or English muffins.

Amazin' A.M. Pizza

Wisconsin White Cheddar Pizza with Bacon, Walnuts and Sage

PIZZA & PASTA

DEEP DISH PIZZA

25	pounds GOLD MEDAL® H&R All-Purpose Flour	9 1/2	ounces sugar
15	pounds water (variable)	16	ounces corn oil
6 1/2	ounces salt	2	ounces instant yeast

- Place water in mixing bowl.
- Add remaining ingredients (except yeast).
- Blend on low speed for 30-45 seconds. Add instant yeast to center of mixture and continue mixing to full development (8-10 minutes).
- Scale and round into desired size. Cover doughballs lightly with oil and place in covered containers.
- Place into retarder (refrigerator) overnight or until needed (minimum 6 hours, maximum 72 hours).
- Allow doughballs to reach room temperature prior to use (approximately 45-60 minutes).
- Sheet/roll out each dough piece to desired size.
- Place in lightly oiled deep-dish pan (pan sides should be oiled).
- Build up a dough edge along side of pan.
- Let dough rise 15-45 minutes (depending on thickness desired).
- Top and bake in a 450-degree oven until golden brown.

GREEK DEEP DISH PIZZA

Yield: 24 servings
Serving size: 4 ounces

2	pounds JENNIE-O® Hickory Smoked Turkey Breast or JENNIE-O® Ground Turkey	2	eggs, slightly beaten
		1/2	cup chopped onions
1 1/2	pounds complete biscuit mix (dry)	1/2	pound Feta cheese, divided
1 1/2	cups water	1	pound fresh tomato, sliced
1	tablespoon ground cumin	1/2	teaspoon salt
1	tablespoon crushed oregano	1/2	teaspoon pepper
1/2	teaspoon garlic powder	1/4	cup Italian dressing
1 1/2	pounds spinach, thawed and chopped	1/2	cup drained and sliced ripe olives

- For hickory smoked turkey: shave and coarsely chop. For ground turkey: sauté, drain and crumble.
- Combine biscuit mix with water. Lightly oil shallow baking pan or pie plate and place crust.
- Place turkey over biscuit crust.
- Combine cumin, oregano and garlic powder; sprinkle spice mixture over turkey.
- Drain thawed spinach and squeeze out moisture; combine spinach with egg, onion and half the crumbled cheese; spread evenly over ingredients in pan.
- Arrange tomato slices over pizza; sprinkle tomatoes with salt and pepper and drizzle dressing over top. Bake in preheated 400-degree oven for 30-40 minutes until crust is browned and mixture reaches 165 degrees.
- Top with remaining Feta cheese and olives. Let stand 15 minutes before portioning.

DIJON PEPPERS, SPINACH AND GARLIC WHOLE WHEAT PIZZA

Yield: 6 (12") pizzas

2	pounds skim ricotta cheese, drained	1/4	cup sliced garlic (1/8")
1	teaspoon dried basil	6	RICH'S Pizza Shells
1	teaspoon dried McCORMICK Oregano Leaf	1/2	cup cornmeal
1/2	teaspoon McCORMICK Black Pepper	18	ounces wilted spinach
3/4	cup GREY POUPON® Country Dijon Mustard, divided	6	ounces part-skim mozzarella, grated
	Vegetable oil spray	1/4	cup grated Parmesan cheese
3/4	pound red and yellow peppers, sliced		

- For the Dijon-ricotta cheese spread, combine the ricotta cheese, basil, oregano, black pepper and 1/2 cup Dijon mustard; refrigerate until needed for service.
- In a hot, non-stick pan or cast iron skillet sprayed lightly with vegetable oil spray, sear the peppers; lower the heat to medium-low and sauté the garlic until golden. Toss the peppers and garlic with the remaining 1/4 cup Dijon mustard and refrigerate until needed for service.
- For each serving, place a pizza shell on a cornmeal-dusted sheet pan and spread with 1/3 cup Dijon-ricotta cheese. Top with 3 ounces spinach, 1 ounce mozzarella cheese, 1 ounce reserved peppers and 1 teaspoon Parmesan cheese. Heat at 425 degrees until cheese is melted.

Pizza & Pasta

PALLADINO'S ONE-TWO PUNCH PIZZA

Yield: 1 (12") pizza

2	tablespoons chopped garlic	1/4	teaspoon sugar
1	tablespoon olive oil	1/8	teaspoon McCORMICK Black Pepper
1	cup chopped roasted red bell peppers		Dash red pepper, crushed
1/3	cup ANGELA MIA® PRIMA CHOICE® Concentrated Crushed Tomatoes	2/3	cup HUNT'S California Dried Tomato Bits
		1	prepared RICH'S Pizza Shell
1/3	cup ANGELA MIA® Extra Heavy Pizza Sauce	3/4	cup grated mozzarella cheese
1/3	cup water	3/4	cup grated Colby cheese
3/4	teaspoon McCORMICK Oregano	3/4	cup grated Swiss cheese
1/2	teaspoon grated Parmesan cheese	6	ounces boneless, skinless chicken breasts, grilled and cut in strips
1/2	teaspoon McCORMICK Basil		
1/2	teaspoon granulated garlic	1/4	cup HUNT'S California Dried Tomatoes in Oil
1/4	teaspoon salt		Basil, chopped

- ❖ In skillet, sauté garlic in oil; stir in peppers. In food processor, process mixture until pureed. Set aside.
- ❖ In bowl, combine crushed tomatoes, pizza sauce, water, oregano, Parmesan cheese, basil, garlic, salt, sugar, black pepper, red pepper, tomato bits and reserved bell pepper mixture; mix well.
- ❖ On each pizza shell, spread 12 ounces sauce mixture.
- ❖ Top each pizza with 3 ounces each: mozzarella, Colby and Swiss cheese.
- ❖ Top each pizza with 6 ounces chicken and 2 ounces tomatoes in oil.
- ❖ Sprinkle with basil.
- ❖ Bake until cheese is melted and crust is golden.

BARBECUED CHICKEN PIZZA

Yield: 1 (12") pizza

3-4	ounces boneless, skinless chicken breast halves	1	cup DOLE® Pineapple Tidbits or Pineapple Cubes, drained
6	tablespoons barbecue sauce, divided	2 1/2	ounces roasted red bell pepper, cut in strips
1	cup pizza sauce	6	ounces mozzarella cheese, grated
1	12" pizza shell	2	tablespoons chopped parsley

- ❖ Pound chicken until flat. Arrange chicken on broiler pan or grill. Brush chicken with 1 tablespoon barbecue sauce. Broil 3 minutes; turn chicken and brush with 1 tablespoon barbecue sauce. Broil 3 additional minutes or until chicken is no longer pink in center. Cut chicken into strips.
- ❖ Spoon pizza sauce over crust. Top with chicken strips, pineapple and red bell pepper. Drizzle 4 tablespoons barbecue sauce over pizza; sprinkle with cheese and parsley.
- ❖ Bake at 425 degrees 20-25 minutes or until crust is golden brown.

ROASTED GARLIC SHRIMP PIZZA

Yield: 4 servings

Yield: 1 3/4 cups

1	12" pizza shell (fresh or frozen)		*Roasted Garlic Cream Sauce*
1	cup *Roasted Garlic Cream Sauce*	1/2	stick butter
6	plum tomatoes, peeled and diced	3	tablespoons all-purpose flour
12	large spinach leaves, slivered	1 1/2	cups milk, heated
8	ounces BEE GEE Cooked Salad Shrimp	2	cloves garlic, roasted and pureed
	BELLAGIO Extra Virgin Olive Oil		Salt
1 1/2	cups grated mozzarella cheese		White pepper
	Cracked black pepper		Nutmeg

- ❖ Place crust on prepared pizza pan and cover with Roasted Garlic Cream Sauce, leaving a 1/2" rim.
- ❖ Sprinkle tomatoes and spinach evenly.
- ❖ Add shrimp and drizzle with olive oil.
- ❖ Sprinkle with mozzarella cheese; garnish with cracked black pepper.
- ❖ Bake at 450 degrees 15-20 minutes or until crust is golden brown.

Roasted Garlic Cream Sauce

- ❖ Melt butter in a saucepan. Add flour and cook over low heat for 3-4 minutes. Slowly add heated milk and whisk.
- ❖ Continue whisking until sauce thickens. Add roasted garlic and spices to taste; allow to cool.

Tyson's Pizza Pounder

Buffalo Pizza

TYSON'S PIZZA POUNDER

Yield: 10 servings
Serving size: 16 ounces

<u>Pizza Sauce</u>
5	cups commercial pizza sauce
2	tablespoons Italian seasoning blend

30	TYSON Spicy Breast Tenderloins (#2556)
10	7" prebaked pizza shells
5	cups marinated, quartered artichoke hearts (drained)
3 1/2	cups roasted red bell pepper strips
2 1/2	cups sliced black olives
5	cups grated mozzarella cheese
	Minced parsley

❖ To make pizza sauce, combine sauce and Italian seasoning in bowl. Mix well, cover and chill.
❖ Deep-fry frozen breast tenderloins at 350 degrees for 3-5 minutes. Remove from fryer. Drain. Keep warm.
❖ To assemble pizza to order: Spread 1/4 cup reserved pizza sauce on shell. Add 1/2 cup artichokes, 1/3 cup red bell pepper strips, 1/4 cup olives and 1/4 cup mozzarella.
❖ Place 3 breast tenderloins on pizza, and sprinkle 1/4 cup mozzarella over chicken. Bake in preheated oven at 400 degrees for 15-20 minutes. Remove from oven.
❖ Sprinkle with parsley and serve immediately.

BUFFALO PIZZA

Yield: 1 (12") pizza

4	ounces RYKOFF-SEXTON Chicken Breasts, seasoned, grilled and sliced		1	prepared RICH'S Pizza Shell
			1 1/2	ounces red onion, cut into rings
1/3	cup DR. WING'S BUFFALO SAUCE® (Surefire or Wildfire)		1	cup grated LA BELLA VILLA Mozzarella Cheese
1/2	cup ANGELA MIA® PRIMA CHOICE® Concentrated Crushed Tomatoes		1/2	cup crumbled CROSS VALLEY FARMS Bleu Cheese

❖ In bowl, combine chicken and 1 ounce buffalo sauce; mix well.
❖ In separate bowl, combine tomatoes and remaining buffalo sauce; mix well.
❖ Spread sauce on pizza shell.
❖ Top each pizza with chicken mixture, onion, mozzarella cheese and bleu cheese.
❖ Bake until cheese is melted and crust is golden.

PIZZA & PASTA

PASTA PRIMAVERA

Yield: 7 3/4 quarts

2	cups thinly sliced onions	8	ounces yellow squash, sliced
1/3	cup oil	1	#10 can RAGU® Recipe Selection Hearty Tomato Sauce
2	cups sliced carrots	1	teaspoon basil
6	garlic cloves, finely chopped	1/2	teaspoon pepper
8	ounces broccoli flowerets	2 1/2	pounds cut fusilli, cooked al dente
8	ounces zucchini, sliced		

- ❖ Cook and stir onions in hot oil. Add carrots and garlic. Cook and stir.
- ❖ Add broccoli, zucchini and squash. Cook and stir until vegetables are tender.
- ❖ Add tomato sauce, basil and pepper. Bring to a boil, then simmer 5 minutes.
- ❖ Combine hot pasta and sauce.

CHICKEN-SPINACH LASAGNA

Yield: 24 servings

White Chicken Sauce Layer

3/4	cup butter
3/4	cup all-purpose flour
3	cups milk
1	(49 1/2 ounce) can SWEET SUE Chicken Broth, divided
1	(50 ounce) can SWEET SUE Deluxe Boned Chicken
3	tablespoons McCORMICK Fennel Seed

Spinach Layer

4	pounds RYKOFF-SEXTON Frozen Spinach, chopped
16	ounces lowfat cream cheese, softened
1	cup ricotta cheese
1	tablespoon McCORMICK Italian Seasoning
	Salt
	Pepper
2	pounds uncooked SAN GIORGIO Lasagna Noodles
24	ounces LA BELLA VILLA Mozzarella Cheese, sliced
4	cups freshly grated Parmesan cheese

- ❖ White chicken sauce layer: Melt butter over medium heat. Stir in flour and cook 1 minute, stirring constantly. Gradually stir in milk and 3 cups of chicken broth. Add boned chicken and fennel, heating thoroughly; hold.
- ❖ Spinach layer: Thaw spinach and drain, squeezing out moisture. Combine spinach, cheeses, Italian seasonings, salt, pepper and 1 1/2 cups of chicken broth. Mix well and hold.
- ❖ Layer lasagna as follows: Put a small amount of white chicken sauce in bottom of 12" x 20" x 2" pan. Add a layer of uncooked noodles. Sprinkle noodles with 1/2 cup chicken broth. Add more white chicken sauce; layer mozzarella slices, Parmesan, spinach, uncooked noodles, sprinkled with 1/2 cup broth, white chicken sauce, etc., ending with cheeses. Bake covered at 350 degrees for 45 minutes. Remove cover the last 10 minutes of baking time to brown cheeses.

PASTA SALAD PICCATA

Yield: 75 servings
Serving size: 8 ounces

10	pounds uncooked penne rigati
9	pounds, 10 ounces boneless, skinless RYKOFF-SEXTON Chicken Breasts
1	quart, 12 ounces dry white wine or chicken broth
1	quart, 12 ounces water

Dressing

1 1/2	quarts BELLAGIO Olive or Vegetable Oil
19	ounces white wine vinegar or white vinegar
10	ounces RYKOFF-SEXTON Lemon Juice
1/2	ounce garlic, minced
	Salt
	Ground pepper
5	pounds sweet red pepper, coarsely chopped
2	pounds, 4 ounces green onion, sliced
1	bunch parsley, chopped
1	pound, 4 ounces capers (optional)

- ❖ Cook pasta according to the cooking instructions on case; drain. Rinse with cold water to cool quickly; drain well.
- ❖ In large stockpot, cover chicken with wine and water (add additional water, if needed, to cover). Simmer until thoroughly cooked; drain. Cool chicken; cut into thin strips.
- ❖ In large bowl, whisk dressing ingredients together.
- ❖ Toss cooled pasta, chicken, dressing and remaining ingredients until thoroughly combined. Cover and refrigerate.

Spinach Lasagna Magnifico

Easy & Lean Fettuccine

SPINACH LASAGNA MAGNIFICO

Yield: 1 half-size hotel pan

3	pounds ricotta cheese		WESSON® Pan Coating
1 1/4	cups chopped RYKOFF-SEXTON Frozen Spinach, thawed and squeezed dry	2	pounds, 8 ounces HEALTHY CHOICE® Garlic and Herb Pasta Sauce
3/4	cup egg product	12	SAN GIORGIO Lasagna Noodles, cooked and drained
1	tablespoon McCORMICK Garlic Powder	1 1/2	cups grated reduced-calorie mozzarella cheese
2	teaspoons McCORMICK Black Pepper		Additional sauce (optional)
1/2	teaspoon ground nutmeg		

- In bowl, combine ricotta cheese, spinach, egg product, garlic powder, pepper and nutmeg; mix well.
- Spray pan with pan coating.
- For small batch: Spread 4 ounces sauce on bottom of pan, layer 4 noodles, half cheese filling and 12 ounces sauce; repeat layers ending with sauce.
- For large batch: Spread 8 ounces sauce on bottom of each pan; layer 6 noodles, half cheese filling and 1 pound, 8 ounces sauce; repeat layers ending with sauce.
- Sprinkle mozzarella cheese on top, dividing evenly for large batch.
- Bake in preheated 350-degree oven 1 hour. Let stand 10 minutes before serving.
- Serve with additional sauce, if desired.

SEAFOOD LASAGNA

Yield: 6 servings

4	ounces uncooked SAN GIORGIO Lasagna Noodles	1/4	cup freshly grated Parmesan cheese
28	ounces spaghetti sauce (jar or favorite homemade recipe)	1	tablespoon minced fresh parsley
6	ounces cooked BEE GEE Salad Shrimp	1/8	teaspoon pepper
4	ounces SEA LEGS Surimi Seafood, thinly sliced	2/3	cup grated lowfat mozzarella cheese
1/2	cup lowfat ricotta cheese		

- Heat oven to 375 degrees. Prepare lasagna according to package directions.
- Empty spaghetti sauce into saucepan and simmer for 10 minutes until thickened and reduced to about 3 cups; stir in shrimp and surimi seafood. Combine ricotta cheese, Parmesan cheese, parsley and pepper in small bowl.
- To assemble lasagna, place half of noodles in 8" x 8" casserole dish. Top with half of seafood sauce; drop half of ricotta mixture by small teaspoonfuls on top. Sprinkle with half of mozzarella cheese. Repeat layers. Bake for 35 minutes or until bubbly. Let stand 10 minutes before cutting.

EASY & LEAN FETTUCCINE

Yield: 25 servings
Serving size: 1 cup

1/4	cup BELLAGIO Olive or Vegetable Oil	1	cup evaporated skim milk
2	tablespoons minced garlic	1/2	cup GREY POUPON Mustard
1 1/2	pounds fresh mushrooms, sliced	1/2	teaspoon McCORMICK Salt
1	pound RYKOFF-SEXTON Frozen Peas, thawed	1/2	teaspoon McCORMICK Pepper
3	pounds JENNIE-O® Oven Roasted Half Turkey Breast*	1	tablespoon McCORMICK Parsley Flakes
1 1/2	quarts poultry broth	1 1/2	pounds uncooked SAN GIORGIO Fettuccine
3/4	cup cornstarch	1	cup grated Parmesan cheese

- ❖ Heat oil; sauté garlic and mushrooms until tender. Add peas and cook an additional 2-3 minutes. Set aside.
- ❖ Cut turkey into strips 1/4" x 2 1/2." Set aside.
- ❖ Bring poultry broth to a boil.
- ❖ Combine cornstarch with a small amount of water. Stir until smooth.
- ❖ Add cornstarch mixture, milk and mustard to heated broth. Simmer until thickened to thin, white sauce consistency, stirring constantly. Add salt, pepper and parsley.
- ❖ Meanwhile, cook fettuccine in boiling water until tender; drain.
- ❖ Combine cooked fettuccine, sauce, vegetables and turkey. Place in counter pans. Top with Parmesan cheese. Broil until cheese browns.

*Can substitute boneless skin-on breast.

TORTELLINI WITH HOT SAUSAGE AND FENNEL

Yield: 2 servings

1/2	pound LA BELLA VILLA Hot Bulk Italian Sausage	1/2	cup chicken broth
1/2	cup finely chopped onion	1/4	cup heavy cream
1	clove garlic, minced	1/2	pound SAN GIORGIO Rigatoni
1	tablespoon BELLAGIO Olive Oil		Salt
1	cup chopped red bell pepper		Pepper
2	cups thinly sliced fennel bulb		Freshly grated Parmesan cheese
1/3	cup dry white wine	1/4	cup minced fresh parsley leaves

- ❖ Cook sausage; crumble, drain and set aside. Sauté onion and garlic in oil until tender, add pepper and fennel. Sauté 5 minutes more. Add wine and broth, bring to boil and simmer 5 minutes.
- ❖ Add cream, boil until thick and reduced by 1/3. Add cooked rigatoni. Toss with fennel and sausage mixture. Add salt and pepper to taste, sprinkle with Parmesan and garnish with parsley.

LINGUINE AND PESTO SAUCE

Yield: 4 servings

2	cups packed fresh spinach	2	tablespoons walnuts
1/4	cup fresh parsley sprigs	1/2	teaspoon salt
1/4	cup grated Parmesan cheese	1/8	teaspoon McCORMICK Pepper
2	cloves garlic	8	ounces uncooked SAN GIORGIO Linguine
2	tablespoons olive oil		

- ❖ Combine all ingredients except linguine in food processor or blender. Process or blend until mixture is smooth. Meanwhile, cook linguine according to package directions; drain.
- ❖ Immediately toss hot linguine with sauce; serve.

TEXAS STYLE TWIRLS

Yield: 100 servings
Serving size: 8 ounces

10	pounds, 6 ounces lean ground beef	3/4	ounce McCORMICK Dried Parsley
5	cups chopped onion	3	tablespoons McCORMICK Oregano Leaves
1/2	ounce McCORMICK Garlic Powder		McCORMICK Salt
12	pounds, 14 ounces RYKOFF-SEXTON Tomato Sauce		McCORMICK Ground Cayenne Pepper
10	pounds whole canned tomatoes, drained and chopped	10	pounds uncooked SAN GIORGIO Macaroni Spirals
5	pounds, 6 ounces barbecue sauce		

- ❖ In large stockpot, cook meat, onion and garlic powder until onion is tender and meat is brown.
- ❖ Add tomato sauce, whole tomatoes, barbecue sauce and seasonings; simmer 30 minutes or until sauce thickens.
- ❖ Cook pasta according to directions; drain. Stir together hot pasta and sauce.

Fettuccini and Ham Salad

Broccoli Linguine and Wisconsin Pepato with Wisconsin Parmesan Cream Sauce

FETTUCCINI AND HAM SALAD

Yield: 4 servings

1/2	cup diagonally sliced carrots	1/4	cup tarragon vinegar
8	ounces SAN GIORGIO Spinach Fettuccini	2	tablespoons BELLAGIO Olive Oil
12	ounces CURE 81® Ham	1/8	teaspoon dried tarragon leaves
1	small onion, sliced and separated into rings	1/8	teaspoon dried basil leaves

- Place carrots in steamer basket over water. Cook 10-12 minutes or until crisp-tender.
- Cook fettuccini according to package directions.
- In large bowl, combine ham, carrots, fettuccini and onion.
- In jar with tight-fitting lid, combine vinegar, oil, tarragon and basil; cover and shake well. Pour over fettuccini mixture. Toss gently to coat.
- Chill 2-4 hours. Toss again before serving.

BROCCOLI LINGUINE AND WISCONSIN PEPATO WITH WISCONSIN PARMESAN CREAM SAUCE

Yield: 8 servings
Serving size: 16 ounces

1 1/2	tablespoons minced fresh garlic	3	cups grated Wisconsin Parmesan cheese
1/4	cup butter	1 1/2	pounds uncooked SAN GIORGIO Linguine
1/4	cup all-purpose flour	1 1/2	pounds RYKOFF-SEXTON Broccoli Flowerets, blanched
1	quart half and half	4	ounces walnut pieces
1/4	cup pesto	8	ounces Wisconsin Pepato cheese, matchstick cut
1 1/2	teaspoons McCORMICK Ground White Pepper		Garlic bread
1 1/2	teaspoons dried thyme leaves		

- Sauté garlic in melted butter. Blend in flour; cook 1 minute.
- Stir in half and half, pesto and seasonings. Bring to boil, stirring occasionally. Blend in Wisconsin Parmesan Cheese. Cook 1 minute or until melted.
- Cook linguine in plenty of boiling water. Drain.
- Toss hot pasta and hot broccoli with cheese sauce. Divide onto serving plates. Top with walnuts and 1 ounce Wisconsin Pepato cheese. Serve with garlic bread.

Variations: Brunch—Add smoked salmon. For the cheese, use shaved Wisconsin Asiago.
Midscale—Instead of linguine, use spaghetti; instead of broccoli, use a blend of frozen vegetables.
Blue it—For the cheese, use crumbled Wisconsin Gorgonzola.
Upscale—For the cheese, use grated Wisconsin Gruyere and toss with grated Black Forest ham.

Vegetable Patch Pasta Salad

VEGETABLE PATCH PASTA SALAD

Yield: 25 servings
Serving size: 1 cup

2½	pounds JENNIE-O® Cooked Turkey Breast, Grand Champion or Oven Roasted		
3	tablespoons RYKOFF-SEXTON Lemon Juice		
1	pound raditore or rotini pasta		
1	pound fresh broccoli flowerets		
8	ounces frozen sugar snap peas, thawed		
1	pound red or yellow cherry tomatoes		
1	cup toasted walnuts (optional)		

Creamy Basil Dressing

1	pound plain lowfat yogurt
1	cup reduced-calorie mayonnaise
¾	cup grated Parmesan cheese
2	tablespoons dried basil
1	tablespoon minced garlic
1½	teaspoons McCORMICK Pepper

❖ Cut turkey breast into ½" cubes. Toss with lemon juice.
❖ Cook pasta in boiling water until tender. Cool under cold running water; drain well.
❖ Cut broccoli flowerets into bite-sized pieces. Steam broccoli 1 minute. Cool under cold running water; drain well.
❖ Combine pasta, broccoli, peas and tomatoes.
❖ In separate container, combine dressing ingredients. Pour dressing over salad mixture and toss to coat.
❖ Garnish with toasted chopped walnuts at time of service, if desired.

PASTA CHICKEN SALAD

Yield: 8 servings

8	ounces uncooked SAN GIORGIO Large Shells	½	pound fresh mushrooms, sliced
2	cups cubed cooked chicken (light meat)	1	cup reduced-calorie creamy Italian salad dressing
2	cups fresh raw RYKOFF-SEXTON Broccoli Flowerets	¾	cup skim milk
2	cups chopped fresh raw RYKOFF-SEXTON Cauliflower		Salt
1	cup sliced carrots		Pepper
1	cup sliced green onion		

❖ Cook large shells according to package directions; drain. Cool. (Rinse with cold water to cool quickly; drain well.)
❖ Combine cooled large shells with remaining ingredients and toss lightly. Chill.

PIZZA & PASTA

DESSERTS

Eugene's Shortbread Tea Cookies, page 88

Chocolate Marshmallow Mousse Pie

Cookie Peanut Butter Pie

CHOCOLATE MARSHMALLOW MOUSSE PIE

Yield: 4 (9") pies

30	ounces cream cheese, softened	3 1/4	quarts prepared whipped topping
1 3/4	cups sugar	7	ounces miniature marshmallows
17	ounces water	25	ounces OREO® Bulk Cookie Pieces, large crunch
15	ounces ROYAL® Instant Chocolate Mousse	4	(9") OREO® Pie Crusts
5	ounces cocoa powder		OREO® Bulk Cookie Pieces, small crunch

❖ Beat cream cheese and sugar with a paddle in a mixing bowl until smooth. Add water, instant chocolate mousse and cocoa powder; mix on low speed for 30 seconds until combined, then on high speed for 3-5 minutes until thickened.

❖ Fold in prepared whipped topping; gently fold in marshmallows and cookie pieces (large crunch). Spoon 8 cups into each pie crust. Garnish with cookie pieces (small crunch).

❖ Refrigerate until firm, about 4 hours.

COOKIE PEANUT BUTTER PIE

Yield: 4 (9") pies

2 1/2	pounds CROSS VALLEY FARMS Cream Cheese, chilled	12	cups prepared RICH's Whipped Topping
3/4	pound chunky peanut butter	4	(9") OREO® Pie Crusts
1 1/2	pounds peanut butter cups	2 1/4	pounds crumbled brownies
10	ounces unsalted, roasted peanuts		Chocolate fudge topping
3 1/2	pounds sweetened, condensed milk		OREO® Bulk Cookie Pieces, medium crunch
1 1/2	pounds OREO® Bulk Cookie Pieces, large crunch		Peanut butter cups, coarsely chopped

❖ In a mixer bowl, combine cream cheese, chunky peanut butter, peanut butter cups, peanuts and sweetened condensed milk; mix until smooth. Fold in cookie pieces (large crunch) until incorporated. Take one half mixture and fold in whipped topping; set aside.

❖ Spread remaining mixture evenly in pie crusts, sprinkle with crumbled brownies and top with remaining peanut butter mixture. Drizzle fudge topping over pies and refrigerate 8 hours or overnight. Garnish with cookie pieces (medium crunch) and peanut butter cups.

DESSERTS

CHOCOLATE TRUFFLES

1	pound PILLSBURY Milk Chocolate RTS Icing
2/3	cup sifted powdered sugar*
1	cup PILLSBURY H & R All-Purpose Flour
1/2	cup coconut*
2/3	cup finely chopped nuts*
	Cocoa*
	Candy sprinkles*

❖ Mix all of the above together until well-combined.
❖ Roll mixture by hand into large, marble-sized balls. Roll balls in additional powdered sugar, coconut, chopped nuts, cocoa or sprinkles. Place on sheet pan; chill until firm.

*Additional amount of ingredient needed for rolling finished balls.

CAPPUCCINO CHOCOLATA AMANTE

Yield: 11 (9") amantes

1	(6 pound) box PILLSBURY Deluxe Brownie Mix
1	teaspoon ground cinnamon
2 3/4	cups hot coffee
2	tablespoons vanilla
2	cups chocolate chips (12 ounces)
	Cocoa Dust
1/2	cup PILLSBURY RTS Icing (any flavor)
	Sliced almonds
	Chocolate shavings
	Raspberries
	Chocolate syrup

<u>Cocoa Dust</u>

1	cup powdered sugar
1/2	cup cornstarch
2	tablespoons unsweetened cocoa
2	teaspoons ground cinnamon

❖ Place brownie mix and cinnamon in mixer bowl; dry blend at low speed using a paddle for 1 minute.
❖ Add coffee and vanilla. Mix at low speed for 1 minute; scrape bowl and paddle. Continue mixing at low speed for 1 1/2 minutes, adding chocolate chips the last 30 seconds.
❖ Draw 9" circles on paper-lined sheet pans or prepare 9" layer cake pans (paper-lined or grease bottoms only). Portion and spread 2, #8 (approximately 4 ounces) dippers of batter onto each drawn circle or into each cake pan.
❖ Bake at 350 degrees in a conventional oven (300 degrees in a convection oven) about 20-30 minutes. Do not over bake. Cool completely before topping.
❖ Dust each 9" round with Cocoa Dust. Spread with desired flavor of icing. Garnish with sliced almonds, chocolate shavings and raspberries. Drizzle with chocolate syrup. Cut each amante into 8 wedges.

<u>Cocoa Dust</u>
❖ Combine all ingredients; mix well.

Chocolate Truffles

Cappuccino Chocolata Amante

DESSERTS

Holiday Eggnog Cake

Chocolate Angel Food "Yule Log"

HOLIDAY EGGNOG CAKE

7	cups water
1/4	cup rum extract
1	box GOLD MEDAL® Yellow Cake Mix
1	tablespoon ground McCORMICK Nutmeg

<u>Glaze</u>
3   cups GOLD MEDAL® RTS Vanilla Icing*

Yield: 3 (10") bundt cakes, 36 servings or 1 full sheet cake, 64 servings
Serving size: (for sheet cake) 2" x 3"

<u>Decorator Icing</u>
2   cups GOLD MEDAL® RTS Vanilla Icing*
1   cup powdered sugar
           Liquid paste color, green
           Red hot candies

- Pour 1/2 total water and rum extract into mixer bowl.
- Add total amount of mix and nutmeg. Mix using a paddle attachment on medium speed for 2 minutes.
- Add remaining water gradually while mixing on low speed. Stop mixer. Scrape bowl and paddle.
- Mix batter on low speed for 2 minutes. Do not over mix.
- Deposit 2 pounds, 14 ounces batter into greased and floured 10" bundt pan or total batter weight into 16" x 24" full sheet pan with pan extenders. If pan extenders are not available, use 8 pounds of batter per sheet pan. Make cupcakes from extra batter.
- For convection oven, bake at 300 degrees: bundt pan for 35-40 minutes, sheet pan for 25-30 minutes. Rotate sheet pans 1/2 turn after 10 minutes of baking. For standard oven, bake at 350 degrees: bundt pan for 30-40 minutes, sheet pan for 21-30 minutes.
- To make glaze, place total amount of icing in a small saucepan. Heat icing over low heat until glaze is free flowing.
- To make decorator icing, combine vanilla icing and powdered sugar. Mix until smooth. Add green liquid paste until desired shade of green is obtained. Place icing in pastry bag with a leaf tip.

<u>Finishing and merchandising</u>
Bundt cakes: Place warm icing into a parchment icing bag. Cut tip to allow icing to flow freely out of bag (approximately 1/4" from tip of bag). Drizzle glaze randomly over cake top, allowing icing to flow down sides. Garnish cake top with a light dusting of powdered sugar. Pipe three leaves on each cake. Place red hots near leaves as holly berries.

Sheet cakes: Apply approximately 2 pounds of icing over top of sheet cake. Score cake top into desired portion sizes. Pipe a single green leaf on each serving. Place red hot candies near leaf for holly berries.

*GOLD MEDAL® White Icing Mix in Traditional or Buttercreme may be substituted for the RTS icing.

DESSERTS

CHOCOLATE ANGEL FOOD "YULE LOG"

Yield: 2 rolls, 24 servings
Serving size: 1"

2	boxes GOLD MEDAL® Angel Food Cake Mix
2 1/2	cups cool water (approximately 72 degrees)
4	tablespoons cocoa powder

Strawberry Cream Cheese Filling

2 1/2	cups CROSS VALLEY FARMS Cream Cheese (1 pound, 4 ounces), softened
3/4	cup thawed RYKOFF-SEXTON Frozen Strawberries
1/2	cup sifted powdered sugar
	Powdered sugar
1	(11 pound) tub GOLD MEDAL® RTS Chocolate Icing*
3	candy poinsettias (optional)

- *Follow package directions for preparing 2 boxes of cake mix.*
- *Add cocoa powder to cake batter during last minute of mixing.*
- *Pour 1 pound, 8 ounces batter per 16" x 24" paper-lined half sheet pan.*
- *Bake in convection oven at 300 degrees for 15-20 minutes. Bake in standard oven at 350 degrees for 23-28 minutes.*
- *To make strawberry cream cheese filling, combine softened cream cheese with strawberries in mixer bowl. Using a paddle attachment, mix on low speed until smooth. Add powdered sugar gradually and mix thoroughly. Refrigerate until needed.*

Finishing and Merchandising

Lightly sprinkle powdered sugar on top of cooled cake. Place a towel or parchment paper on top of cake and invert. Remove paper liner. Spread approximately 3 cups strawberry filling evenly over top of cake. Grasp upper end of towel or parchment paper and roll cake lengthwise with firm pressure so cake sticks to filling. Wrap cake with towel or parchment. Set cake seam side down. Refrigerate. When thoroughly chilled, remove towel or parchment. Ice cake roll with chocolate icing. Smooth icing with spatula or cake comb to give "tree bark effect." Dust with sifted powdered sugar for snowflake appearance and finish with candy poinsettias. Refrigerate before serving. Dip knife in hot water before slicing to obtain smooth, even slices.

Note: To preserve for later use, wrap finished cake rolls in plastic film and freeze.

*To determine total amount of icing needed, allow 1 1/2-2 pounds icing per cake.

CHOCOLATE CARAMEL PECAN CAKE

Yield: 1 sheet cake, 64 servings or 3 (8") 3-layer cakes, 36 servings
Serving size: (for sheet cake) 2" x 3"

	Cool water (approximately 72 degrees)
1	box GOLD MEDAL® Chocolate Cake Mix
1/2	tub GOLD MEDAL® RTS Chocolate Fudge Icing*
4	cups pecan halves (1 pound), toasted
4 1/2	cups prepared heavy caramel sauce**

- *Pour 1/2 total water into mixer bowl.*
- *Add cake mix. Mix using a paddle attachment on medium speed for 2 minutes.*
- *Add remaining water gradually while mixing on low speed. Stop mixer. Scrape bowl and paddle.*
- *Mix batter on low speed for 2 minutes. Do not over mix.*
- *Pour all batter into 16" x 24," greased and floured sheet pan or 13 ounces per 8" greased and floured layer cake pan.*
- *Bake in convection oven at 300 degrees: sheet pans for 24-29 minutes, layers for 19-24 minutes. Rotate pans 1/2 turn after 10 minutes of baking. Bake in standard oven at 350 degrees: sheet pans for 27-32 minutes; layers for 21-26 minutes.*

Finishing and Merchandising

Sheet cake: Ice sheet cake with approximately 2 pounds of chocolate fudge icing. Sprinkle 3 cups toasted pecan halves over icing. Drizzle cake with 2/3 cup caramel sauce.

Layer cakes: Level cake tops as necessary. Place cake layer on a cake circle. Ice layer with chocolate fudge icing out to cake edges. Sprinkle 1/2 cup toasted pecan halves over icing. Drizzle caramel sauce over pecans, allowing caramel to run down cake sides. Repeat procedure twice to create a 3-layer cake.

*GOLD MEDAL® Chocolate Fudge Icing Mix in Traditional Add Water Only or Buttercream may be substituted for the RTS icing.

**Caramel sauce must be very thick to remain on cake.

DESSERTS

Yule Log

Creamy Bread Pudding

YULE LOG

Yield: 1 Yule Log

2	pints coffee ice cream
2	cups (1 pound, 6 ounces) JHS Cold Fudge Topping (#22100)
5	maraschino cherries, drained (optional)
	Mint leaves (optional)

- Remove ice cream from containers. On foil-lined tray, push wide ends together, forming a log. Use spatula to smooth joined ends. Cover; freeze until firm.
- Working quickly, spread fudge over "log," covering completely.
- Using fork tines, make horizontal lines in fudge to resemble the bark of a tree.
- Cut cherries in half; arrange 3 with mint leaves to resemble holly berries. Make 2-3 "holly" clusters, if desired.

CREAMY BREAD PUDDING

Yield: 15 servings
Serving size: 6 ounces

1 1/2	pounds Granny Smith apples, peeled and thinly sliced		1/4	teaspoon salt
1/2	pound sweet butter, divided		1	quart milk
12	ounces sugar, divided		8	ounces heavy cream
1 1/2	teaspoons ground cinnamon		1	teaspoon vanilla
1/4	cup currants		1	pound PILLSBURY All-Butter Croissants, baked and cut into 1" cubes
6	whole eggs			
3	egg yolks			

- Sauté apples in 1/4 pound sweet butter.
- When apples begin to weep, add 4 ounces sugar and cinnamon. Allow to simmer 5 minutes. Add currants.
- Melt remaining butter and pour into a half-size steam table pan.
- Beat eggs, yolks, remaining sugar and salt.
- Scald milk and heavy cream together.
- Remove from heat and temper in egg mixture; add vanilla.
- In steam table pan, layer egg mixture, croissant cubes and apple mixture.
- Bake at 375 degrees in a conventional oven (325 degrees in a convection oven) in a water bath for about 45 minutes or until custard is set.

Serving suggestions: Serve warm with whipped cream, raspberry sauce and fresh raspberries.

DESSERTS

FUDGE CHEESECAKE BARS

Yield: 64 servings
Serving size: 2" x 3"

1	box GOLD MEDAL® Fudge Nut Bar Filling Mix	3	fresh eggs
	Cool water for filling mix (approximately 72 degrees)	1	tablespoon McCORMICK Vanilla Extract
3	cups CROSS VALLEY FARMS Cream Cheese (1 pound, 8 ounces)	1	box GOLD MEDAL® Fudge Nut Bar Crust Mix
			Cool water for crust mix (approximately 72 degrees)
¾	cup sugar		

- Follow filling mix directions.
- Combine cream cheese, sugar, eggs and vanilla in mixer bowl. Mix using a paddle attachment on medium speed for 2 minutes. Scrape bowl and paddle. Mix an additional 3 minutes on medium until mixture is smooth and well-blended.
- Place dollops of cream cheese mixture randomly over chocolate filling in pan.
- Drag a small knife or metal spatula through cream cheese and chocolate batters to create a marbled effect.
- Prepare crust topping as directed on package. Crumble over filling.
- Bake in convection oven at 300 degrees for 27-30 minutes, rotating pans only if oven has severe hot spots. Bake in standard oven at 350 degrees for 28-31 minutes.

CHOCOLATE RASPBERRY SWEETHEART BROWNIES

Yield: 12 servings
Serving size: 3"

Frosting
1	tablespoon butter
¼	pound semi-sweet chocolate morsels
⅓	cup heavy cream
1	teaspoon McCORMICK Vanilla Extract
½	cup seedless raspberry jam, divided
1	cup sifted powdered sugar

6½	cups prepared fudge brownie batter
1½	cups OREO® Bulk Cookie Pieces, medium crunch, divided

- For frosting, melt butter and chocolate morsels in a heavy-bottomed saucepan over medium-low heat; stir until smooth. Add heavy cream, vanilla and ¼ cup raspberry jam; stir until incorporated. Gradually add sugar and beat until smooth; set aside.
- To prepare brownies, pour half of prepared brownie batter into a lightly greased half hotel pan. Sprinkle with 1 cup cookie pieces and drizzle remaining raspberry jam evenly over cookies. Pour remaining batter over cookies.
- Bake in a 350-degree oven 30 minutes; remove from oven and cool slightly. Spread frosting on warm brownies and sprinkle with remaining cookie pieces. Cool completely and cut into 12 (3") squares.

Note: To substitute prepared frosting, add ¼ cup seedless raspberry jam to 2⅓ cups frosting.

FUDGE BROWNIE COOKIES

Yield: 54 cookies
Serving size: 3"

2	cups cool water
1	(6 pound) box PILLSBURY Deluxe Brownie Mix
	Powdered sugar

- Pour water into mixer bowl; add brownie mix. Mix according to package directions. Chill dough well.
- Drop using a #30 dipper (about 1½ ounces dough) into powdered sugar; coat evenly. Place 24 cookies on each paper-lined sheet pan in a 6 x 4 pattern.
- Bake at 375 degrees in a conventional oven (300 degrees in a convection oven) 11-14 minutes or just until set. Do not over bake.

Desserts

Lemon Cheesecake

Banana Pecan Bread

LEMON CHEESECAKE

Yield: 1 (9") cheesecake, 16 servings (trial recipe)

1	cup NABISCO® Graham Cracker Crumbs	1	cup softened light cream cheese (Neufchatel)
1 1/4	cups sugar, divided	2	tablespoons lemon juice
2	tablespoons melted FLEISCHMANN'S® Margarine	1/2	teaspoon grated lemon peel
3	cups lowfat cottage cheese (1% milkfat)		Lemon slices (optional)
2	cups FLEISCHMANN'S® EGG BEATERS® Real Egg Product		Fresh fruit (optional)

❖ In medium bowl, combine crumbs, 3/4 cup sugar (1/4 cup for trial recipe) and margarine; divide and press onto bottom and 1 1/2 inches up side of 3 lightly-greased springform pans (one 9" pan for trial recipe).
❖ In blender or food processor fitted with steel blade, blend half cottage cheese and 1 cup egg product until smooth, scraping down side of container as necessary; pour into mixer bowl. Repeat with remaining cottage cheese and 1 cup egg product. (Blend 3 cups cottage cheese and 1/2 cup egg product for trial recipe.)
❖ Combine cottage cheese mixture, remaining egg product, remaining sugar, cream cheese, lemon juice and lemon peel; beat on low (speed 1) 2 minutes.
❖ Scrape side and bottom of bowl. Increase speed to medium (speed 2). Beat 8 minutes. Pour into prepared crusts.
❖ Bake at 325 degrees for 1 hour* or until puffed and set.
❖ Cool in pan on wire rack. Chill at least 3 hours.
❖ Cut each cheesecake into 16 wedges. Arrange lemon slices and fresh fruit on each wedge, if desired.

*For convection oven, time and/or temperature may need to be reduced.

BANANA PECAN BREAD

Yield: 1 (9" x 5") loaf (trial recipe)

2	ounces FLEISCHMANN'S® Margarine, softened	1 1/4	pounds bananas, pureed
7	ounces sugar	10	ounces GOLD MEDAL® All-Purpose Flour
1/2	cup FLEISCHMANN'S® EGG BEATERS® Real Egg Product	2	teaspoons GOLD MEDAL® Baking Powder
2	ounces unsweetened applesauce	2	ounces pecans, coarsely chopped
1	teaspoon McCORMICK Vanilla Extract	1/2	cup raisins (packed)

❖ In large mixing bowl, cream margarine and sugar. Beat in egg product, applesauce, vanilla extract and banana puree; set aside.
❖ Thoroughly mix flour and baking powder, add to reserved liquid ingredients and mix until flour is moistened.
❖ Fold in pecans and raisins; do not over mix.
❖ Divide batter into 2 greased and floured 9" x 5" loaf pans (1 greased and floured pan for trial recipe); bake in a 325-degree oven for approximately 80 minutes, until a toothpick inserted in the center comes out clean. Remove from oven and allow to cool before releasing from pan. Slice each loaf into 12 pieces.

DESSERTS

Cinnamon Raisin Bagel Pudding with Caramel Sauce

German Chocolate Bagel

CINNAMON RAISIN BAGEL PUDDING WITH CARAMEL SAUCE

Yield: 16 servings

1	quart milk
4	cups light cream or half and half, divided
6	large eggs, slightly beaten
1½	cups sugar
2	teaspoons vanilla extract
6	ARNIE's Cinnamon Raisin Bagels
	Rich Caramel Sauce

Rich Caramel Sauce

¾	cup butter
¾	cup brown sugar
¾	cup sugar
¾	cup whipping cream
2	teaspoons vanilla extract

❖ Combine milk, 1 cup cream (or half and half), eggs, sugar and vanilla in large mixing bowl; mix well.

❖ Cut or tear bagels into 1" pieces. Add to milk mixture; mix well. Pour into well-sprayed, half steam table pan. Cover with aluminum foil. Refrigerate 4 hours or overnight.

❖ Bake until set or knife inserted near center comes out clean. In a convection oven, bake at 325 degrees, covered 30 minutes, then, uncovered 15 minutes. In conventional oven, bake at 350 degrees, 60-65 minutes, uncovered. Transfer to steam table. Hold, uncovered, on medium (#5 setting) up to 1 hour.

❖ To serve, cut into 2¾" x 2¼" pieces. Pour 3 tablespoons cream (or half and half) into each bowl. Top with bread pudding and 3 tablespoons Rich Caramel Sauce or prepared caramel sauce.

Note: Great use for day-old bagels.

Rich Caramel Sauce

❖ Combine all ingredients in 2-quart heavy saucepan. Bring to boil over medium heat, stirring constantly. Simmer 10-12 minutes or until slightly thickened. Cool 20-30 minutes before serving.

GERMAN CHOCOLATE BAGEL

Yield: 12 servings
Serving size: 1 bagel half

¾	cup sugar
6	tablespoons butter
¼	cup evaporated milk
2	egg yolks
1	teaspoon McCORMICK Vanilla Extract
1	cup flaked coconut

¾	cup chopped pecans
6	ARNIE'S Plain or Egg Bagels, baked and split
12	ounces semi-sweet chocolate morsels, melted
	Fresh mint springs (optional)
	Fresh raspberries (optional)

❖ Combine sugar, butter, milk, egg yolks and vanilla in 2-quart heavy saucepan. Cook over medium heat until mixture thickens, about 6 minutes, stirring constantly. Remove from heat. Stir in coconut and pecans. Refrigerate until thick enough to spread, about 30 minutes.

❖ Spread cut sides of bagels with melted chocolate. Let stand 10 minutes to firm. Lightly spread with coconut mixture. Broil just until topping is hot, about 1 minute.

❖ Garnish with fresh mint sprigs and a few fresh raspberries.

Desserts

GLAZED BLUEBERRY CREAM CHEESE SCONES

Yield: 82 scones
Serving size: 2 ounces

1 1/2	cups sugar
2	cups CROSS VALLEY FARMS Cream Cheese (1 pound), softened
5	cups cold water or milk (50 degrees)
	Full box GOLD MEDAL® Buttermilk Biscuit Mix
2 2/3	cups frozen and rinsed blueberries

<u>Powdered Sugar Glaze</u>

4	cups powdered sugar
2	tablespoons corn syrup
1/4	cup hot water (120 degrees)
1/2	teaspoon McCORMICK Vanilla Extract

❖ Combine sugar and cream cheese in mixing bowl. Mix until smooth. Add cold liquid. Mix until smooth.
❖ Add biscuit mix. Mix using a rubber spatula until a soft dough forms. Fold blueberries into fully mixed dough.
❖ Deposit No. 20 scoop of batter (2 ounces) on a 16" x 24" greased or paper-lined sheet pan.
❖ Bake in convection oven at 400 degrees for 8-10 minutes, rotating pans 1/2 turn after 4 minutes of baking. Bake in standard oven at 450 degrees for 12-14 minutes.
❖ To make glaze, combine all ingredients in mixing bowl. Mix using a rubber spatula or wire whip until blended. Brush tops of warm scones with glaze.

EUGENE'S SHORTBREAD TEA COOKIES

1	(5 pound) box PILLSBURY Deluxe White Cake Mix*
2	cups (1 pound) unsalted butter or margarine, softened
2	tablespoons vanilla
2	cups chopped pecans**
2	cups (9 ounces) powdered sugar
3/4	cup (3 ounces) cornstarch

❖ Place cake mix, butter and vanilla in mixer bowl. Mix at low speed using a paddle for 2 minutes; scrape bowl and paddle. Add pecans and mix at low speed for 1 minute.
❖ Portion using a #40 dipper (about 1 ounce dough) onto paper-lined sheet pans in a 6 x 4 pattern; flatten each to a 1 1/2"-2" round.
❖ Bake at 350 degrees in a conventional oven (300 degrees in a convection oven) 8-12 minutes or until light golden brown. Cool. Combine powdered sugar and cornstarch; roll cookies in mixture, coating evenly.

Variation: Dip cooled, baked cookies in melted semi-sweet chocolate instead of rolling in powdered sugar. Coat entire cookie or half of each cookie.

*1 (5 pound) box PILLSBURY Deluxe Yellow Cake Mix or 1 (4 pound, 8 ounce) box PILLSBURY Plus White or Yellow Cake Mix can be substituted for the PILLSBURY Deluxe White Cake Mix.

**May substitute the following for pecans: 2 cups chopped walnuts, hazelnuts or almonds; 3 cups flaked coconut or 3 cups chocolate, butterscotch or peanut butter chips.

Glazed Blueberry Cream Cheese Scones

Eugene's Shortbread Tea Cookies

DESSERTS

Caramel Apple Pie

Lowfat Peach Cobbler Cake

CARAMEL APPLE PIE

Yield: 2 pies

12	ounces CROSS VALLEY FARMS Cream Cheese, softened
2	eggs
1	tablespoon McCORMICK Vanilla
1/3	cup sugar
2	tablespoons all-purpose flour
2	(6 ounce) prepared NABISCO Graham Cracker Pie Crusts
24	ounces (1/3 tray) STOUFFER'S® Escalloped Apples, thawed
2/3	cup caramel topping
1	teaspoon McCORMICK Cinnamon

- Preheat standard oven to 375 degrees.
- In mixing bowl, combine softened cream cheese, eggs, vanilla, sugar and flour. Beat until smooth. Divide mixture between pie crusts.
- Combine apples, caramel topping and cinnamon. Gently spoon over cream cheese mixture to maintain two distinct layers on each pie.
- Bake 45-50 minutes or until apples bubble up around pie edges.
- Serve at room temperature. Promptly store leftover pie in refrigerator.

LOWFAT PEACH COBBLER CAKE

Yield: 24 servings
Serving size: 2 3/4" x 2 3/4"

1	#10 can RYKOFF-SEXTON Sliced Peaches, with juice
1/2	box GOLD MEDAL® Lowfat Variety Muffin Mix
1 1/2	cups brown sugar
2	teaspoons McCORMICK Cinnamon
24	small peaches

- Drain peaches, reserving 3 cups juice.
- Combine muffin mix, brown sugar and cinnamon in a mixer bowl. Mix with paddle attachment on low speed for 2 minutes.
- Add reserved peach juice and peaches. Mix on low speed just enough to moisten dry ingredients (approximately 20 seconds).
- Pour total amount of batter into a lightly sprayed 11" x 17" x 2" baking pan or 12" x 20" x 2" steam table pan.
- Bake in convection oven at 300 degrees for 45-55 minutes or standard oven at 350 degrees for 55-65 minutes.
- To finish, cut cake into 24 (4" x 6") servings. Garnish with dollop of whipped topping. Place small peach slice on whipped topping.

Desserts

Mighty '50s Malted Bundt Cake

Raspberry Fizz

MIGHTY '50s MALTED BUNDT CAKE

Yield: 3 bundt cakes

Cake
2 1/2	cups cool water, first
1	(5 pound) box PILLSBURY Deluxe Yellow Cake Mix
2	tablespoons vanilla extract
1/2	cup unsweetened cocoa powder
4	cups cool water, second
4 1/2	cups malted milk ball candies (cake or 48 candies)

Caramel Sauce
2	cups butter
6	cups firmly packed brown sugar
1/2	cup light corn syrup
2	cups whipping cream
1	quart whipped topping
48	malted milk ball candies (optional)

- Pour first water into mixer bowl; add cake mix, vanilla and cocoa.
- Mix on medium speed using a paddle for 1 minute.
- Add second water gradually over 1 minute while mixing at low speed.
- Scrape bowl and paddle; mix at low speed 2 minutes.
- Scale 3 cups batter into each of 3 well-greased and floured 12-cup bundt pans;* place 16 malted milk ball candies (2 1/2 ounces) over cake batter in each pan.
- Bake at 350 degrees in standard oven (300-degree convection oven) about 65-75 minutes; invert onto wire rack. Cool completely.
- To make caramel sauce, melt butter in saucepan; stir in brown sugar and corn syrup. Bring to boil and cook until sugar is dissolved, stirring constantly. Stir in whipping cream and bring to boil again; remove from heat.
- Ladle each bundt cake with 3/4 cup caramel sauce.
- Upon slicing bundt cakes for service, ladle each slice with 2 tablespoons caramel sauce; garnish with whipped topping and top with a malted milk ball candy, if desired.

*May use 10" angel food tube pans.

RASPBERRY FIZZ

Yield: 1 serving
Serving size: 16 ounces

1/4	cup raspberry sauce
1/4	pound frozen raspberries
1/3	cup milk
1/2	cup vanilla frozen yogurt
1/3	cup OREO® Bulk Cookie Pieces, small crunch
2/3	cup soda water
	Whole OREO® Cookies

- In blender, combine raspberry sauce, frozen raspberries, milk and frozen yogurt; blend until smooth.
- Add cookie pieces and blend until smooth.
- Pour into a 16-ounce glass and splash with soda water; garnish with whole cookies.

DESSERTS

MOCHA ANGEL FOOD CAKE

Yield: 1 (10") angel food cake

<u>Cake</u>
1	cup cold, strong coffee
1	tablespoon unsweetened cocoa
1	(14 ounce) box PILLSBURY Angel Food Cake Mix

<u>Glaze</u>
2	tablespoons hot, strong coffee, divided
1	tablespoon light corn syrup
1	tablespoon unsweetened cocoa
1 1/4	cups powdered sugar

Chocolate curls (optional)

- *Pour cold coffee into mixer bowl. Combine cocoa and cake mix; place in mixer bowl.*
- *Mix at low speed using a wire whip for 1 minute; scrape bowl and wipe whip. Continue mixing for 2 minutes at medium speed. (If mixing by hand, mix for 3 minutes with a whisk.)*
- *Pour batter into an ungreased, 10" tube pan.*
- *Bake at 325 degrees in standard oven (300-degree convection oven) for 40-60 minutes. Invert cake and cool at least 1 hour.*
- *After cake has completely cooled, run a small, thin knife around edge of pan; remove cake from pan.*
- *Place 1 tablespoon hot coffee and remaining glaze ingredients in small mixing bowl; mix until well-combined. Add remaining hot coffee, one teaspoon at a time, until glaze is of desired consistency.*
- *Drizzle cake with glaze. Garnish with chocolate curls, if desired.*

MUDSLIDE CAPPUCCINO

Yield: 1 serving
Serving size: 16 ounces

1	cup coffee ice cream
1/2	cup milk
3/4	cup OREO® Bulk Cookie Pieces, medium crunch
1	teaspoon instant espresso powder
	Prepared RICH'S Whipped Topping
	McCORMICK Ground Cinnamon
	Wet walnut topping

- *In blender, blend coffee ice cream and milk until smooth.*
- *Add cookie pieces and instant espresso powder; blend until smooth.*
- *Pour into a 16-ounce glass and garnish with whipped topping, cinnamon and wet walnut topping.*

THE RAPTOR'S REVENGE

Yield: 12 servings

12	chocolate brownies* (2" x 2" x 3/4")
1	quart chocolate ice cream
3	cups marshmallow fluff, warmed
1 1/2	cups chocolate syrup
3/4	pound OREO® Bulk Cookie Pieces, medium crunch

- *For each serving, place a brownie in a banana split dish or in an 8-ounce sherbet dish, then place one #16 scoop of chocolate ice cream on brownie.*
- *Drizzle with 1 ounce each of marshmallow fluff and chocolate syrup.*
- *Garnish with 1 1/4 cups cookie pieces.*

OREO® Brownies can be used instead of chocolate brownies.

DESSERTS